WEBSITE TIPS & TRICKS

15 LESSONS TO SUPERCHARGE YOUR
AUTHOR WEBSITE

BARB DROZDOWICH

Copyright © 2019 by Barb Drozdowich

All rights reserved.

No part of this book may be reproduced in any form or by any electronic or mechanical means, including information storage and retrieval systems, without written permission from the author, except for the use of brief quotations in a book review.

To the ladies of the Kiss of Death chapter of the RWA who helped fine-tune this book.

CONTENTS

Introduction	vii
Lesson 1 – Terminology	1
Lesson 2 - Findability	7
Lesson 3 – Findability part 2	19
Lesson 4 – Website review	27
Website Tips & Tricks - Marketing Cheat sheet	31
Lesson 5 – Where is content placed on a website?	35
Lesson 6 – What content should be on an Author Website?	41
Lesson 7 - User Experience and Menu Structure	49
Lesson 8 – Themes – What they are and How to choose one	53
Lesson 9 - The Science of Reading for Writers	57
Lesson 10 - How to Create Content that is Connected, Scannable, and Shareable	59
Lesson 11 - How to Wrangle Pictures	67
Lesson 12 – How to "see" your audience	73
Lesson 13 - Safety & Security	83
Lesson 14 - Followers, Subscribers, etc.	91
Lesson 15 - Develop a Plan Going Forward	101
Conclusion	107
Glossary	109
About the Author	113
Also by Barb Drozdowich	115

INTRODUCTION

An author's website—certainly at the beginning—is frequently something the author creates by themselves. Whether trying to operate within a tight budget or unwilling to spend money until they really start making money from their books, authors are often shamed into putting something together by themselves. Their fellow writers tell them it is "easy" and they do their best—but they aren't technically skilled or knowledgeable, and they don't really know what they are doing, so they struggle to create something that doesn't look like a toddler put it together.

Does the above paragraph seem overly harsh?

Does this describe you?

Hi there. I'm Barb Drozdowich, an author and a technical author assistant. Over the years I have been working with authors, I know that the above paragraph is true more often than not, and it likely does describe you, as you picked up this book.

Let me explain who I am and why I am the best person to teach you all about your website.

I started my teaching career in 1986—primarily in science and applied science. When I moved across the country in 1995 I found a new job running the technical training department of a bank. Both experiences made me really good at breaking down and explaining complicated subjects something my non-tech author audience appreciates today.

When I left my day job to start raising a family, I began looking around for something to keep my mind going: an intellectual challenge, a technical challenge. A friend suggested I start a blog. I did a bit of investigation, asked for help from a computer-programming student, and was off and blogging. I experimented with a few blogs and in 2010 I started a book blog that kept my interest. I've always been a voracious reader and book blogging allowed me to combine my love of reading with my need for a technical challenge. If only my high school English teachers could see me now...

Although I struggled a bit at the beginning, my technical background helped me learn the world of blogs and websites quite quickly. It wasn't long before I was helping my online friends "fix" their blogs. This started another career as an author virtual assistant focusing on technical tasks and I never did go back to my day job. Now I work from home, primarily serving as a technical trainer to authors.

So, what does this mean for you? It means that I teach various technical tasks that are specific to authors' platforms. It means that I serve as technical virtual assistant. I either teach various tasks, or I do them for the author. It also means that I am responsible (to one extent or another) for maintaining about 75 different websites. The vast majority of these websites are author websites. This quantity of different websites gives me a wide variety of real-life examples.

Because of my experience, my technical bent, as well as my exposure to a large amount of real information about the author world, I look at the author world differently than most authors.

This book is entitled *Website Tips & Tricks: 15 Lessons to Supercharge your Author Website*. I plan to help you learn about websites from the perspective of the needs of an author and to do so in 15 short lessons of focused work. In my mind, the needs of an author are different than the needs of most small businesses. I'm going to have you look in a critical fashion at your own site. This book is aimed at an author who already has a functioning website or blog, but if you don't have a website yet, you can do some of the exercises looking at a friend's website, and planning for your own in the future.

As much as possible, the content of this book will apply to all types of websites. Where there is the need for me to be specific, I will give as many examples as possible.

Let's be clear about a few details. In 2019, anyone selling something needs a presence on the Internet. We can call that presence a website or we can call that presence a blog. As we'll learn, the word website and blog are often used interchangeably.

I am aware we are in the world of authors, not of small businesses. Most readers don't do a Google search when looking for their next read. They are much more likely to search Amazon or Goodreads or even Facebook when trying to decide what to read next. So, I'm sure you're begging to ask the question "Then why do I need a website? Why won't a Facebook Page do?" The short answer is you want a presence on the Internet on real estate **you own**. The longer answer that since it is the year 2019, as an author, you are running a business, and therefore for the sake of validity you need a searchable location on the Internet. Having a website gives you credibility.

Back to the idea of real estate you own, you want a place to store information about you and your books that won't disappear if the platform it is on disappears.

Most of the authors I work with would rather be writing their next book. As a voracious reader I'm totally on board with that philosophy! But for websites and blogs, you need a technical trainer, so I focus on quick and efficient ways to manage technical tasks. I focus on putting authors in control of the boat rather than the boat in control of the author.

The other thing you'll figure out quite quickly is that I don't feel most authors need an overly complicated website. They simply need a place on the Internet to share information about their books. However, that place should be professional looking and should work **for** the author (not the reverse). I have preferences as you'll see as we work our way through the material in this book, but I don't feel that a website so complicated that an author can't manage it (if she chooses) is necessary. Those fancy websites that cost thousands of dollars and do everything including folding the laundry are not necessary in the author world.

If you have a technical bent, I suspect that you have already scoured the Internet and discovered all the content that is covered in this book. The audience for this book is the beginner, the author who may have a website but is somewhat intimidated by the whole situation. The author for whom some patient teaching, some plain English explanation will make the world of difference. If this isn't you, I encourage you to return this book and find a book that will challenge you a bit more.

Lastly, to give you an idea of what we're going to cover in this book, I'll share a brief outline. We will start with the meaning of some words. In my experience, the world of websites is full of foreign-sounding words. It is easier to teach if we're all speaking the same language. In the first block of lessons we're going to learn some technical details about websites. I'm going to get you to start looking at your website with a critical eye. The next block of lessons is going to look at the content of your website. In the third block we're going to talk about making your website more efficient. The last block is going to talk about subscribers and connecting your website to other platforms.

Lots to learn. I look forward to helping you in every way I can.

LESSON 1 – TERMINOLOGY

Welcome to lesson 1! In this lesson we are going to focus on those foreign-sounding words that have to do with websites. As I mentioned in the previous lesson, it's much easier to teach when everybody is speaking the same language. All of the words that we learn today are defined in the "Glossary" at the end of this book. As we learn new words, I will refer you back to the Glossary for reference.

Let's start with words that have to do with your website itself.

The word "**URL**" or "**domain**" refers to the address of your website. Just like the place you live has an address; your website also has an address. This address has a beginning and a middle and an end. It always follows a pattern. A URL or a domain starts with "**http://**" or "**https://**" The next section for an author should be the author's first name and last name. The last section is often ".com" but it can be ".co.uk" or ".com.au" or ".ca" or a couple of other suffixes.

You'll notice that I suggested an author's domain contain their name. We'll talk more about that in a coming lesson. For now, as part of your homework, I want you to determine the domain of your website if you have one.

Although the words "**URL**" and "**domain**" are used interchangeably, they can also have different meanings. Typically, the word **domain** refers to the basic address or the root address of a website or a blog – such as http://barbdrozdowich.com. The word URL, however, can be used to refer to a basic domain as well as the address to a specific place on a website such as http://barbdrozdowich.com/my-books/ or http://barbdrozdowich.com/resources/.

If we go back to the "where you live" analogy, in addition to having an address, you likely also have a structure. You live in a house or an apartment or a townhouse or a condo. Your website is no different. Instead of having rooms it has files. These files have to live somewhere—they have to reside somewhere. The place where these files live is called a "**server**." A server is simply a complicated computer that is connected to the Internet. Although it is possible to have your own server in your house, most people don't. They rent space on a server that is owned by a company. This company is referred to as a "**hosting company.**" You may pay money to a hosting company or your hosting may be free. Examples of hosting companies are GoDaddy, InMotion Hosting and SiteGround to name a few.

All websites are run on what's known as a "**platform.**" A platform is a computer program that takes information in the files and turns it into something visual. Turns it into what we know looks like a website. There are quite a few different platforms that are used to create websites. Some examples are WordPress, Blogger, SquareSpace, Weebly, and Wix, to name a few. If you have a website, what platform do you use? That's the next piece of your homework. See if you can figure out what platform us use to operate your website. At the end of this lesson, you can find a screenshot that will help you quickly determine if you have WordPress.org or WordPress.com

. . .

A website itself has words that are used to refer to various parts or sections of it.

Let's start with the term **"landing page."** The landing page is literally where someone lands when they type in your direct URL or domain. A landing page is often also referred to as the front page or home page of a website.

There are also a selection of words that refer to the various parts of the website. Starting at the top is what we call the **"header."** The header may be text or it may be a graphic. Below that space is typically a line of words that we call the **"menu" (or menu bar)**. The words on the menu can be clicked on to take the reader to other content. The space below the menu is what we call the **"body"** of the website. The body is often divided into two sections. The first being the main part of the body and the second, typically smaller and usually on one side or the other, is called the **"sidebar."** The space below the body is what we call the **"footer."** The footer runs along the bottom of a website. It can contain content or it can be blank. Typically, it is where the copyright statement is found.

Let's talk about the program that you have on your computer that is used to view websites. This program is called a **"browser."** There are many different kinds of browsers. The common ones are: Chrome, Firefox, Safari, and Internet Explorer, to name a few. There are good browsers as far as websites are concerned and not so good browsers. Most people that design websites would prefer that you use Chrome or Firefox to view websites. There can be issues when using Internet Explorer or Safari. You will hear me repeating this information as we go forward. You can't guarantee that what you see using Internet Explorer (for example) is the correct view of a website.

All browser programs retain versions of websites in their memory. This is called **"caching."** A **"cache"** is simply a collection of information about websites that have been viewed on a particular browser. It allows the browser to load information about a website faster. Caching is a good thing and a bad thing. It increases speed of loading for the websites that are commonly viewed, but if changes are being made, this caching function can prevent us from seeing changes.

Lastly, we are going to talk about the words "**website**" and "**blog**." If we go back in history, the word "**website**" typically referred to a site on the Internet that didn't change very often. The word "**blog**," referred to a site on the Internet that was more of a journal and because of this, the content changed frequently. Today these words are used interchangeably. Almost every platform allows the user to have some portion of their site to be static and also have a blog or a changeable component. Because of this, we can direct all traffic from our readers to one URL. They can then use the menu bar to view various parts of the site. More on that in a future lesson.

Let's summarize your homework for today.

Homework #1 - I want you to write down the Domain or URL for your website if you have one. (If you don't have one, use the information from a friend to do your homework.) And keep in mind when I use the word **website** I mean website and/or blog.

Homework #2 - I want you to figure out what platform is being used for your website. (See the hint at the end of this chapter.) The next thing I want you to do is figure out where your site is hosted. Who do you pay money to or what company do you pay money to? If you have a WordPress.com website you will have free hosting and the host is WordPress.com.

Homework #3 - I want you to look at your website and perhaps some of your friends' sites and see if you can figure out the header, the body, the footer, and the sidebar areas for these sites.

. . .

One last thing I want you to do, in preparation for what we're going to learn next, is to look at your website in a variety of different ways. If at all possible, I would like you to look at your website on a big desktop computer screen. Next, I'd like you to look at your website on a laptop computer screen. Next, I'd like you to look at your website on a tablet screen, perhaps something like an iPad. Lastly, I'd like you to look at your website on a smart phone screen. In my experience most people that have a website only look at that site on their own computer and this only gives them one perspective. If you don't have a tablet or a smart phone or a laptop perhaps a family member does; perhaps a friend does. See what you can do to view your website on a variety of different devices, and we will talk about this in the next lesson.

Technical hint: Here's your hint to help you determine if you have a WordPress.com or WordPress.org site.

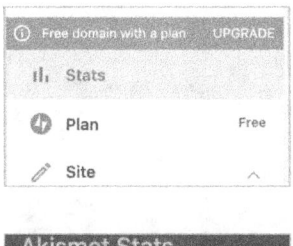

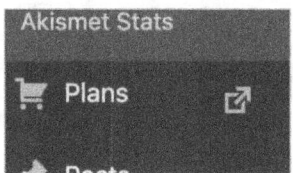

If you have a WordPress.com site, whether you look at the dashboard of the site or click on WP Admin and look at that dashboard, you should be able to spot the word "Plan" or "Plans" on the menu which runs down the left side of your screen. If you can't—you have a WordPress.org site.

LESSON 2 - FINDABILITY

The overarching theme we are going to start today is **Findability**. This lesson has screenshots and specifics I want you to look at and learn from. Get yourself a beverage (my beverage of choice is coffee) and settle in to learn.

We will be talking about Google quite a bit today. Before we wander into the intimidating world of Google—have you Googled yourself lately?

Why not do that before we go any further? Bring up a browser on your computer and type in Google.com to bring up the Google search screen. In the search field, type in your name (or your author name if you are working with a pen name).

What are the results? Did Google list your website on the first or second page? We'll table that information for a bit and go on to a few more details before coming back around to it.

. . .

Google is what's known as a "responsive" search engine program. In other words, it wants to make you happy! It wants to help you find what you are looking for. As a result, it remembers what you have done in the past and tries to respond more accurately if you repeat a search. Because of this, if you have searched yourself repeatedly on Google, Google will get better and better at finding you.

A true test is to use the public library computer or your neighbor/friend's computer—don't log onto anything as yourself and do a Google search for your author name. Are the results different? They might well be.

You'll remember in a previous lesson I said that most readers don't go to Google to find their next read. They don't open a Chrome browser window and search on Google for "great romantic suspense" or "great horror novel" or "educational children's book." It is much more likely that they search Amazon, Kobo, Barnes & Noble, Goodreads or even Facebook, Twitter, or Instagram. So, why pay attention to Google at all?

The short answer is that Google rules the world. They set the rules and they are the monster in the room which enforces the rules. Google is by far the most popular search engine in the world. Regardless of whether a large number of readers will actually search Google for us, we need to be there and be findable if they do.

Part of being findable on Google is abiding by their rules. Google has brought in a number of rules over the last few years that we need to pay attention to.

Rule #1 - Mobile Responsive

Starting in 2015, Google required websites to be "Mobile

Responsive." So...what the heck is "Mobile Responsive" for the non-technical person? And why is it so important?

Mobile Responsive is the ability of a website to reorganize its content and menu line to be small-size user friendly. Google has created a graphic to help with understanding. See it below:

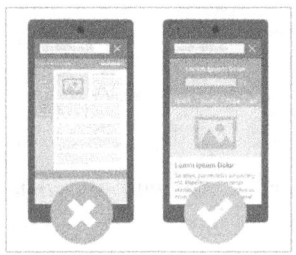

There are two ways that websites can "adjust" for a smaller screen —they can just get smaller to fit or they can completely reorganize their content. Looking at the graphics above, the version on the left is the "get smaller" version. My old eyes can't read content that just gets smaller to fit in the available space :) And don't get me started on trying to get my fingers tapping the right area on a menu line!

When the content is reorganized—as you can see in the right-hand graphic above—the content doesn't become smaller, it moves around. It becomes vertical—the sidebar is no longer on the side; it is viewed under the body content. A picture for a post or page is viewed first with the content below. And although it isn't shown on the graphic above, the menu line is typically converted into an icon with 3 horizontal lines (called the "hamburger menu" or "flyout menu") that can be tapped on to expand to a useable state.

So, the next question is why is Google forcing this? To quote Google:

> "Mobile is changing the world. Today, everyone has smartphones with them, constantly communicating and looking for information. In many countries, the number of smartphones has surpassed the number of personal computers; having a mobile-friendly website has become a critical part of having an online presence."

They then go on to say:

> "In the USA, 94% of people with smartphones search for local information on their phones. Interestingly, 77% of mobile searches occur at home or at work, places where desktop computers are likely to be present."

From my experience, most author websites are actually accessed via a desktop computer—unless the author focuses on a YA or MG audience. However, since Google sets the rules, we must follow them.

Again, to quote Google:

> "Google will be giving preferential search rankings to sites optimized for mobile."

If your website is not mobile responsive, you will not be as visible in a Google search.

. . .

So how do you tell if your site is up to snuff according to Google?

You can use this handy-dandy test site

https://search.google.com/test/mobile-friendly

Assignment #1 - click on that link and test your website's URL to see what Google says about your site and its mobile accessibility.

I'll wait.

What did you find? Is your site mobile friendly? How does your site appear on a mobile device? Is there room for improvement or are you pretty happy with the way it looks? We'll be talking more about this in future lessons, but for now, be aware that the theme that you use for your website is the source of the mobile responsiveness of your site to a large degree. If your theme is old, it is likely not compliant with the current rules.

On to the next topic.

Rule #2 - Page Loading or Loading speed

Earlier this year Google released some research and concluded the following:
   "The average time it takes to fully load the average mobile landing

page is 22 seconds. However, research also indicates 53% of people will leave a mobile page if it takes longer than 3 seconds to load."

Google (and other search engines) penalize sites that load slowly. So do users. If a site loads too slowly, they will give up. You know as well as I do, a voracious reader—a reader determined to find information—will tolerate a lot more than someone searching on their phone for the closest hairdresser.

So, is 3 seconds a hard and fast rule? Not really.

However, you want your site to load as fast as possible.

And yes, like the previous section—I have a website you can go to in order to test your site

https://gtmetrix.com/

Click on the link above and type in your website address or URL. Click on the blue "Analyze" button. It will whirl and think and then it will spit out all sorts of information that likely makes you cross-eyed. You are looking for the information that looks like the graphic below:

The graphic above is from my author website. You'll notice it loads in 2.3 seconds but is given an "F" for a whole bunch of reasons. If you scroll down from the above box on your results, likely the first error that is listed is something about images. We will be spending time on preparing images for your website!

So—do I care that I received an F? Not really, I just want my site to load relatively quickly. And by relatively quick, I mean in under 3 or 4 seconds. How fast does your site load? Take note. We'll come back to this in a future lesson. It is possible to improve on this number fairly easily.

Rule # 3 – SSL (Secure Sockets Layer)

The last requirement to make Google a happy camper is the presence of an SSL.

Last July Google started sanctioning websites that didn't have an SSL.

Most authors really don't want to get into the weeds of technology, so let's define SSL as a function your hosting company puts in place to signal your website has a secure connection to the Internet. It is supposed to give folks peace of mind when they are purchasing from websites.

What does it look like? To easily spot the presence of an SSL, your domain or URL has a "https://" rather than a "http://" at the beginning. The presence of that little "s" has a lot of meaning.

In addition, the browser may add comments.

Here is a site WITH an SSL viewed on a Chrome browser:

🔒 https://bakerviewconsulting.com

Here is a site WITHOUT an SSL:

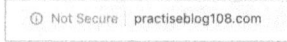

Depending on the computer, the browser being used and the presence or absence of antivirus software, the warning may be much more visible and in fact, access to the website might be blocked.

If your site is missing a SSL, contact your hosting company for help putting this in place. Some hosting companies charge for an SSL, others provide one for free.

Rule #4 Domain/URL

What I've labeled as "Rule #4" isn't as much a rule as it is information. I do, however, find this information to be fairly important.

Did you know that many people will try to find a website by simply bringing up a browser window and typing the name of the company (or in our case, author) followed by ".com" and hitting enter?

Likewise, if Google is trying to find something for a searcher, frequently the first place it will look is for a matching URL or Domain. Because of this, having a domain that matches a potential search gives a huge advantage. And having a domain that matches your author name makes it easier for your readers to find your website.

I am well aware that by marrying my lovely husband, I went from being Barb Smith to having the more unique name of Barb

Drozdowich. As a result, I have never been confronted with trying to choose a domain for a common name. People can't spell my last name—and sometimes I can't spell my last name, but no one else reserved http://barbdrozdowich.com before I did. If your name is more common, you likely found that you had to be creative when choosing a domain name. You might have had to add the word "Author" or "Writer" or "Writes" after your name to find an available domain.

We're going to talk about two aspects of a domain name in this section:
   1) matching
   2) multiples

Let me explain.

1) Matching
    Does the URL for your site match your author name? Or is it some version of your name? If we ignore the addition of the word "Author" or "Writer," can one of your readers hold one of your books (or their Kindle) in one hand and type what they see on your book cover into Google and come up with your website? Or is there a mismatch? In my case—what if my author name was B.E. Drozdowich and my domain was http://barbdrozdowich.com? How would my readers figure that out? Some would, but you want the two to match as closely as possible. You want to make it as easy as possible for your readers to find you.

> **Technical Note:** If your current domain doesn't exactly match your author name, consider registering a second domain which is an exact match in addition to what you have. It is possible to

have more than one domain pointed at one website in almost all cases.

2) Multiples

If you have multiple websites, how does your reader choose which one to click on? Years ago, authors were encouraged to have both a website and a blog—separate entities. This resulted in two entries in Google for one person. Confusing for readers. I always suggest that everything be combined into one site. You want things to be as simple as possible for readers searching for you!

As we approach the end of a content-heavy lesson, I want you to make a list of things that you found through today's exercises. Things that perhaps need to change. Things which need further attention. Some of these will be resolved in future lessons, but make notes as you go.

Your last bit of homework is back to the beginning of this lesson. Remember I suggested you Google yourself? I want you to take a screenshot of what you see— or if you prefer—write the information down. Mine is pictured below:

> Barb Drozdowich - Author
> https://barbdrozdowich.com/ ▼
> Barb Drozdowich has worked with non-technical authors for years & understands how to break complex topics down using non-technical language. She has .

We will start from this point in the next lesson.

Homework for this lesson:

#1 – Using the link provided, check to see if your site is mobile responsive.

#2 – Using the link provided, check to see how fast your website loads—or what the page load speed is.

#3 – Check to see if you have an SSL for your website.

#4 – Check to see if your domain/URL matches your author name. If not, think about adding a new domain to your website.

LESSON 3 – FINDABILITY PART 2

Continuing with the subject of Findability…
Before we start with today's information, notice the set of videos— screencasts—as part of this lesson. I like to show step-by-step instructions for rather technical information. Today's lesson includes five "how-to" screencasts.

I'll be around to help sort out any issues that arise accessing these videos.

Before we start in on this lesson, I want to say a few words about networking. Networking is a skill most professionals master in the real world, but authors struggle with it in the online world. Yes, the topic of this course is to supercharge your website, but we need to learn to draw traffic to our websites. To make our websites into the central hub of our communications with readers. As we will discuss throughout these lessons, supercharging a website involves steps that, on the surface, have nothing to do with the website itself, but have a lot to do with the topic of networking.

In today's lesson, we are going to continue with the subject of findability and turn our attention to locations readers can find us and follow links back to our website.

. . .

What does your Google snippet look like?

We ended the last lesson with a request to screen shot or copy what your Google snippet looks like. To refresh your memory, mine looks like this:

> Barb Drozdowich - Author
> https://barbdrozdowich.com/ ▼
> Barb Drozdowich has worked with non-technical authors for years & understands how to break complex topics down using non-technical language. She has ...

A Google snippet is made up of a title/description in purple, a hyperlink in green and the description in black. Is your blurb helpful? You'll notice that mine is truncated—it cuts off at 156 characters. I guess I need to work on my blurb as well as you do.

Google is a funny duck. Unless it is fed information, it picks and chooses information from a variety of sources. We like to feed this information to Google rather than leaving it to chance.

Ideally, you want your Google listing to be accurate but also be helpful to searchers who are trying to understand who you are and what you write—all in 156 characters.

We are going to talk about how to force the content of your Google snippet by supplying your website with some information. Before we do that, I want you to take a piece of paper—or a computer screen—and create the content, the description of your website you want to add—all 156 characters! Perhaps Google some of YOUR favorite authors to see what they are sharing as part of their blurbs.

Once you have something you are happy with, it needs to be put in place. Keep in mind, this isn't a perfect science, but you can tip the odds in your favor by taking a few steps.

All the platforms offer the ability to add a description or an "excerpt" to a page. This information is added as extra information for a page, or in the settings section for a page. To put in place, look at the information for the home page of your website, and find the excerpt or description field and enter the 156 characters you have put together to describe you and your writing. If your website is on

WordPress.org, I suggest using a SEO plugin like Yoast which will allow for a "meta description" to be added.

Of course your website appears on Google, but where else? A lot of places, like in the back matter of your books, on your Goodreads Author Page, your Amazon Author Page, and on social media. The next few paragraphs will address placement of your website information in these places.

Website information in the back of books

Staying with the subject of findability, in addition to finding you on Google, readers also "find" you through information in the back matter of your books. Having an author bio as well as contact points is a time-honored tradition in publishing. I don't want you to go on memory, pull out one of your books, or perhaps open a file on your computer, and see what exists in the back of your books—both print and e-book. (If you haven't published yet, pull a paperback book off a bookshelf from one of your favorite authors and then look at some selections on a Kindle app.) Are there clickable links? Is the URL spelled out?

Let's talk about some technical aspects to this before we move on. Stating the obvious, most of us who are published have print books as well as e-books, either Kindle or ePub or both. I think it's safe to say that most of us are very familiar with print books, but not all authors have made the leap to reading digitally. If you are not very familiar with digital versions of your book, consider this your chance to become familiar.

There are probably hundreds of different ways to read an electronic book. From standalone e-readers, such as a Kindle or a Kobo reader, to a phone or tablet, or a laptop or desktop computer—the examples are endless. To add to this, not all e-readers are equal. My well-used iPad with its overstuffed Kindle app has more skills than my daughter's basic Kindle. My iPad connects to the Internet and has browser capabilities. My daughter's Kindle does not connect to the Internet with browser capabilities and has no other capabilities than the ability to display the text of the book.

> **Technical note:** There are many different e-readers available on the market. For the sake of my example of a Basic Kindle, I am referring to Amazon's most popular Kindle, the bottom of their product line, the cheapest Kindle available. And yes, there are many different Kindles with many different capabilities. Keep in mind that Amazon claims to have sold tens of millions of Kindles since they first entered the market in 2007.

Logically, what I can do on my iPad is not the same as what my daughter can do on her Kindle. On my iPad, while reading the book, I can tap on a hyperlink and view a website on the Internet. On my daughter's Kindle, I can see a hyperlink but I can't do anything with it.

Taking this knowledge, you should understand that a website which exists as a hyperlink, can easily be accessed while reading my iPad, but not from my daughter's Kindle. What this means is if your website exists as an embedded link that looks like this: Author website, readers on a basic Kindle can't access that link and don't know what the URL is because it is embedded.

Because of this, always make sure that links are written out in full for better clarity. (example: Author website: barbdrozdowich.com) You can still hyperlink them, but for readers using basic e-readers, give them information they can follow up on via their desktop computer.

Let's move the discussion to our print books. Look at the information in the back matter of your print book. Is the direct URL typed out or is there just a general statement encouraging readers to visit a website?

Little details like this can make a big difference when networking with readers. We want to be as helpful as possible and capture their interest in joining us in other ways when they are (hopefully) excited about our books and eager to learn more.

In addition to providing a link to our website, authors are often advised to place links to a mailing list in the back matter of our books also. Although our topic is not mailing lists, the same principle applies—spell out the link. Be helpful

Website information on Goodreads

Goodreads is the site that authors seem to either love or hate. I'm in the category of those who love Goodreads. The voracious reader in me just LOVES to wallow in all that book-loving energy! However, since I teach a course on Goodreads I am well aware that the site itself is somewhat like a rabbit's warren. A bit off-putting to people who are not technical.

The thing with Goodreads is that not only are there 75 million account holders, but it is owned by Amazon. Every book that is published on Amazon eventually ends up being listed on Goodreads.

Because there are 75 million readers on Goodreads, it is essential that you provide as much information as possible to help readers make a buying decision. One of those things that you can do once your book has been published, is connect to your blog's feed to your author profile. Most people are aware that they can list the URL of a website as part of an author's profile information and do that, but not all are aware of the extra ability to connect with readers provided for those who have blogs.

> **Note:** This function is only available to those who have blogs. If you have a website builder site, it likely doesn't have a blog function.

So, is this a big deal? Sometimes yes; sometimes no. I see a huge positive effect from having readers on Goodreads able to access my blog posts. In my mind, if it only sells a small handful of books, it's a good use of time on my behalf to enter the information on Goodreads.

For those who aren't familiar with a blog's feed URL—it is typically your domain (or URL) with /feed/ added at the end. My feed URL for my author site would be http://barbdrozdowich/feed

To find the appropriate area to enter this information, log into your Goodreads account. Click on your picture in the upper right and choose Author Dashboard from the choices. From this point, click on Edit my Author Profile in the upper right and then look for the Edit Blog link and enter the feed information.

Note – adding a blog's feed is a power that only published authors can do. If you haven't published yet, store this information away for when your book has been published.

Website information on Amazon

Most of us are aware that our primary point-of-sale is Amazon. The other thing that most of us are aware of is that the information provided to readers differs across different versions of Amazon. So for example what I see on Amazon.ca about my books is different than what I see on Amazon.com about my books.

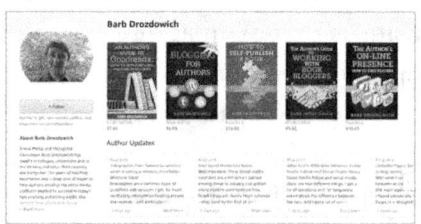

In the above graphic, you can see what my author page looks like on Amazon.com. Amazon allows authors to include a profile picture, a short bio, and connect the feed to their blog. As you can see in the above graphic the last four blog posts from my blog are visible to anyone looking at my books on my author page.

This is a positive and a negative. I tend to blog regularly so anyone seeing this information will realize that the blog posts are relatively current. If you only blog once or twice a year this also will be visible.

One principle that we will come back to frequently in this course is accentuate the positives and hide the negatives. If you only blog once or twice a year don't hookup your blog feed to Amazon and broadcast that information to every reader that visits your Amazon Author Page. If you are going to blog regularly, feel free to share that information with readers.

The starting point for entering this information is via **Author Central**. The URL is: https://authorcentral.amazon.com/gp/home

Sign into this site using your Amazon/KDP credentials. Click on the Author Page link and enter your blog's feed URL in the appropriate field.

> **Note** – an Author Central account is only available to a published author. If you haven't published yet, store this information away for action once your book has been published.

Website information on social media

All social media platforms allow you to create a short bio and enter a website URL.

Take a few moments and check right now to make sure this information is available on all the social media platforms that you have.

One of the things that people don't necessarily realize about social media platforms is that they also can serve as search engines. Just like we bring up Google.com and search for the closest hairdresser, the same thing can be done on most of the various social media sites. I admit that my preference is to search on Google, but folks who spend the majority of their time on Facebook would search Facebook before they would search Google. The same can be said of Twitter or Instagram.

Although we assume that readers are going to find us primarily through Amazon or another book retailer, Google, or in the back matter of our books, in fact we can be found in a variety of different ways.

Regardless of how our readers try to find us, let's attempt to be as helpful as possible.

Today's homework:

1) See if you can enter information in the appropriate area for your platform to force your Google snippet.

2) Have a look at the information in the back matter of your books. Look at the link to your website, etc. and see if it is as helpful as possible and if not, make changes where necessary.

3) Enter your blog's feed URL in Goodreads if applicable.

4) Add your blog's feed URL to your Amazon Author page if applicable.

5) Have a look at your bio information on all social media platforms you participate in and adjust if necessary.

That's it for today's lesson. In the next lesson we're going to look at the content on our websites.

LESSON 4 – WEBSITE REVIEW

In today's lesson we're going to start looking at the content of your website. For those of you who haven't created a website yet, choose a friend's website and do the exercises on that site.

An overarching theme that we will stay with through the next few lessons is "hide the negatives; accentuate the positives." This is a theme that I've mentioned several times so far. In one of the examples, I suggested that if you aren't planning on blogging that you don't display that by hooking up a blog feed to your Amazon author page. There's no hard and fast rule that says an author needs to blog; however, if you're not going to blog very regularly you should take steps to minimize that fact.

What else do I mean by this? Some of the examples are obvious, such as the blog feed and Amazon example above. Other examples are: If you only have three subscribers to your blog don't advertise that fact. If you don't spend any time on Twitter, don't embed a Twitter stream on your blog which makes that obvious.

If we look at the positives, I think you want to avoid language like "future author" or "aspiring author." If you haven't published something yet, perhaps refer to yourself as a Writer. Kind of splitting hairs, but that label might seem more truthful to you. Share positive quotes from reviews of your books—don't share the less than stellar ones. Make sure everything "works" on your website.

Another overarching theme I will come back to frequently is to be as helpful as possible to your readers. You can do this in a number of ways. You can provide a book detail page with as many buy links as possible. If you write in a series, you can help your readers understand which books belong in which series. If you are collecting names for a mailing list, be clear about what people are signing up for.

People lead busy lives. We are always in a rush. Readers are no different. They are looking for information about you and perhaps your books. You want to make this as easy for them to find as possible. We talked about some of this information in the previous lessons. In this lesson we're going to build on that by looking at the content of your website. I'll give you a bit of theory, some activities to do, and then we will build on this information with the next lesson.

To continue with the theme of people and busy lives, your website has, experts say, up to 7 seconds to capture their interest. Some experts predict more time; some predict less. A portion of that 7 seconds will be taken up by the time that your site takes to load, the rest of the time will be taken up by a visitor to your website figuring out if they are in the right place. If they are in the right place, hopefully visitors will look further and spend more time on your website.

If I list the top five reasons people leave a website, they are (in no particular order):

1) They don't feel they are in the right place.
2) The site isn't usable—they can't find a menu line, navigation isn't obvious.
3) The site takes too long to load.
4) The design or the navigation is too complicated.
5) The site is too difficult to use/view on a smaller device.

In previous lessons we talked about #3 and #5 when I had you do the page loading speed test and the mobile friendly test.

We're going to look at, and if necessary, change content on your website to address #1, #2 and #4 today and in the next lesson.

There is a famous survey that was carried out quite a few years ago using jars of jam. The researchers created two different displays. The first display showed four or five different types of jam—all the jars were the same size and all on sale for the same price. The second display showed two dozen different types of jam, all on sale but at different prices and the jars were all different sizes.

The display with only four or five different types of jam sold significantly more jars of jam than the larger display did. It didn't matter the placement of the store geographically, the size of the store, the placement of the display within the store. The conclusion that was made was when you give people too many choices they don't make any choice at all.

The same can apply to websites. This little bit of science refers to item 4 from the list above. More on that in a bit.

If we go back to the exercise of looking at your website on a mobile device, a tablet, and a larger screen like a laptop screen or a desktop screen, we refer to everything that is visible without scrolling as being "above the fold." Not only are people busy, but they are also lazy. Many will **not** scroll to see what is "below the fold."

For an author, above the fold needs to be your name and some way of identifying who you are. That can be done by using words—for example "Barb Drozdowich - technical trainer and author." It can be done using words and pictures or graphics. The words can be your author name, and the picture or graphic can show book covers, or it can be something that sets the tone—typically of the genre you write. Even if you haven't published yet, you can use this graphic to convey genre to a visitor.

Your homework for this lesson is to look at your website (or a friend's website) hopefully on a number of different screen sizes.

Homework task #1 – Looking at your website, can a visitor to your website identify you and what genre you write without scrolling? Can they determine if they have found the right website? Take some notes.

Homework task #2 - Does your menu line give visitors too many choices? A menu line should aim for no more than 5 or 6 primary choices.

Homework task #3 - Look at the whole website—do you see any negatives you want to hide? Make note of them (or change them if you know how). Click on all the links, look at all the pages. Make sure everything works. For example, if your website has a link to a Facebook page, make sure it connects to Facebook. If you have links to Amazon for your books, make sure they connect to the right spot.

Homework task #4 - Many authors struggle with what content to put on their websites - how to talk to their audience. We are going to be talking about this more in future lessons. To help you frame your thoughts, I've included a **Marketing Cheat Sheet**. It is a modified version of what I was given by my traditional publisher in preparation of publishing my first book with them. I was required to completely fill out all the information, but I now use it as an exercise in a number of the classes I teach because it is thought provoking. I'm not requiring you to answer all the questions. Answer the questions and see if it helps you collect your thoughts about you and your books/writing.

Homework task #5 – Who are your competitors? Take some time and go searching on Amazon. Make a list of authors/books who are similar to your book(s) or to books you are creating.

WEBSITE TIPS & TRICKS - MARKETING CHEAT SHEET

Target Market

1. Describe your ideal reader (age, gender, education, geographical location).
2. Describe specific groups of buyers, e.g., teachers of a textbook.
3. Describe the primary need(s) of your target market and how does your book satisfy those needs.
4. What factors and emotions are likely to influence buying decisions?
5. How are you going to reach your target market?

Analysis of Competition

1. Who is your competition?

2. How is your competition who have top-selling books pricing their books?
3. What is your competition doing well—or better than you?
4. Where is your competition struggling? Where can you do better? Where can you improve on what your competition is doing?

Marketing Strategy

1. How will branding play a role in helping you sell books?
2. How will you position yourself among the competition (low price vs. premium price)?
3. What kind of reputation do you want your book(s) to have? How do you want it (them) to be seen in relation to other similar books?

Action Plan

1. What print products will you use? Bookmarks, posters?
2. How will you use your website/blog to promote your book/build relationships with readers?
3. Will you use speaking engagements?
4. Will you use webinars or online courses?
5. What social networks will you use?
6. What off-line marketing tactics will you use?

Summary
4 Ps of Marketing

1. **Product** – Synopsis/blurb, physical description, benefits.
2. **Price** – What price do you choose? What are the plans for sales/discounts?
3. **Promotion** – Summarize your key marketing tactics and tools—public speaking, social media, blogging, etc.
4. **Placement** – What marketplaces will carry your book? Will you sell in person? Will you sell on your website? Through what distribution services?

LESSON 5 – WHERE IS CONTENT PLACED ON A WEBSITE?

As I've mentioned in previous lessons, in my experience, authors tend to be a bit fuzzy about terminology. This creates apprehension with respect to technical subjects and interferes with the learning process. We've worked quite a bit on demystifying the unfamiliar words during this course. This lesson will continue with the demystifying process.

The words that we're going to talk about in today's lesson are:

1. Page
2. Blog Post
3. Sidebar/Footer

In Lesson 2 we talked about the various parts of the website. We defined header, body, footer, and sidebar. These are places on a website that content can be placed. Identifying the places in terms of the geography or structure of a website is helpful, but we also need to define the logistics of how to get content in these various locations.

The places that you have available to you on your website will be determined by the platform you have decided to use and also the theme that you have put in place. We haven't talked a lot about themes yet, but we will in a future lesson. For now, let's define a theme as a collection of coding that controls the overall look and feel of the website. It controls the subdivision of the various geographical or structural parts of a website, the fonts, the colors, and the formatting.

All platforms have the ability to add Pages, most of them have the ability to add Blog Posts, and Sidebar/Footer areas are often determined by the platform and the theme.

In this lesson we're going to talk about these three possible areas where content can be placed. We're going to talk about the intent of these locations and we're also going to talk about what's normal or what's expected.

Page

A Page is a section of the website that contains content. It can contain text (which can be formatted), pictures or other graphics, embedded videos and embedded functionalities. On all platforms a Page is meant to be a static part of a website. Typically, a Page is connected to the menu bar or navigation bar to allow for easy access by visitors to the site. An example of a Page for an author website would be an "About me" page or a "Books" page. We'll talk about details of this sort of content in a future lesson.

Blog Post

A Blog Post or as it's commonly referred to "Post," looks very similar to a Page in terms of its structure. It can contain text (that can be formatted), pictures or other graphics, embedded videos and other embedded functionalities. Where it differs from a Page is its intent. A Post is meant to be part of the serial record of a website. It is meant to be displayed in date order one Post after another.

On the surface, it is sometimes difficult to determine the difference between a Page and a Blog Post, but when entering this information through the dashboard of your website there is a distinct difference.

At this point I'll encourage you to log in to your website and look at the labels that are available. Depending on what platform you're using, you will see an entry for Pages and you may see an entry for Posts or Blog Posts. Information that is intended to be static or of a more permanent nature is placed on a Page. Content that is meant to be serial in nature, or perhaps viewed as periodic updates or additions, is placed on Posts or Blog Posts.

In future lessons we will talk about how to set up the navigation structure of your website to enable accessing information in these two different locations.

Let's move on to the Sidebar/Footer areas. Almost all platforms allow for a footer area, but generally speaking the theme that you choose will determine whether or not a sidebar area is available. In terms of the geography or structure, the footer area is found at the bottom of the website. The sidebar area is often associated with the blog and is typically found on the right or the left side of the body of a website. In terms of the intent, these two spaces are meant to hold ancillary material.

The footer holds, if nothing else, the copyright statement for the website. In many cases it also contains a menu, which is a repeat of the upper menu. The sidebar is the area of a website that holds bits and pieces of information or functionality in terms of decreasing importance. In other words, the information at the top of the sidebar should be more important than the information at the bottom. As an author, it is more important that people follow you on social media and buy your books than see that you are a member of RWA or Sisters in Crime.

In future lessons, we'll talk more about how our visitors consume the content on our website, and we'll talk about the concept of "above the fold." To give you a sneak peek, many visitors to your website will only view what they can see without scrolling, and they will simply scan this.

Directing your attention back to the dashboard of your website, where do we find access to the sidebars and footer areas? This will differ from platform to platform.

If you are using WordPress.com look for WP Admin. Click on it and then click on Appearance and then Widgets.

WordPress.org is similar. Click on Appearance and then Widgets.

With Wix, click on "Edit the site" and then edit the section you want to change. The footer will be found at the bottom of every page.

For Weebly sites, click on "Build" and then adjust the section of content you want. The footer will be found at the bottom of each page.

SquareSpace operates in a similar fashion to both WIX and Weebly. Find the space you want to adjust and change the content.

. . .

Your homework for this lesson is to become familiar with the capabilities of your website. Where is the access for Pages? Do you have the ability to enter Blog Posts? Where are the sidebar/footer areas modified? If you haven't already, play with what can be done with content in these various areas.

LESSON 6 – WHAT CONTENT SHOULD BE ON AN AUTHOR WEBSITE?

Author websites exist to serve the needs of readers. What do readers want when they visit an author's website?

Priorities are:
   - Find out more about the author
   - Learn about books/find out about future books/find out where books are available
   - Read intriguing insights from the author on blog posts
   - Contact the author/find other places the author can be found

The longer you can keep someone on a website, the more likely they are to take actions you want them to take. Because of this, we are going to spend the next few lessons looking at the user experience, talking about the content on your website, and lining up strategies to engage readers.

. . .

Let's start with what readers are seeking.

1) More information about the author

Remember, one of the ways readers find an author website is when they finish reading a book and are excited to find out more. They either use links in the back of the book, or Google and find an author's website. Most websites, regardless of the focus, have an "About Me" page. I don't care what the title is—it doesn't have to be "About Me." It can say "About Barb" or "Meet the Author." Whatever title is chosen, it should be clear what the content of the page will be.

An "About Me" page should be a combination of a bio, a welcome note and a "why I write what I do." It should have a friendly tone and encourage readers to read further. For example, invite them to look at the "Book" page or some other section of the website. It also typically has a picture of the author.

Homework #1 – Take another look at the content on this page for your website. See if you want to rework it a bit. (If you don't have a website yet, take this opportunity to create the page from scratch.)

2) Learn more about the author's book(s)

The people who read this book tend to be at a variety of points in their career—some are yet to publish; some are multi-published, and some are somewhere in the middle. Let's see if I can be all-encompassing in our discussion of books.

In a previous lesson I encouraged you to avoid terms like "aspiring writer" and just use "writer." With respect to books, if you have a book reasonably close to being published, talk about it specifically. If you are a long way from being published, talk about your writing interests more generally. If you are yet to be published perhaps use a title of "writing interests" or something similar. On this page you can share information about what you like to write—what genres, what themes or tropes. Share with the potential audience information about what is coming in the future.

If you are published, you want to use the label of "Books(s)." In fact, if you have published more than one book, you will want to create a series of pages for your books. In the next lesson, I will be talking about how to set up a menu structure for your website. In this lesson we're just going to talk about the information needed by readers and worry about connecting it in the next lesson.

I suggest that each book you publish should have its own page. This page should show the title, the cover graphic, the book's blurb, links to everywhere the book can be purchased, social proof, and possibly an excerpt. This page can be referred to as a "Book Details" page or a "Book Sales" page. The whole purpose of this page is to be attractive to readers and encourage sales. Because that is the purpose, I encourage including more than just the book cover blurb and purchase or buy links. Let readers know what others have thought of your book (social proof). If these thoughts come from other bloggers, link to their blog or website. Similarly, including a short excerpt or the first chapter encourages readers to give the book a test drive of a sort.

If you write books in series, create a "Series" page that allows a collection point of all books contained in this series. Perhaps this page can have a basic outline of the series, as well as connection points to each "Book Details" page.

There are many examples we can emulate. Here are a few of my favorites:

https://www.jillshalvis.com/
https://lynnrayeharris.com/
https://pilkey.com
https://kids.jamespatterson.com/
https://markjdawson.com/

All of these authors have a slightly different presentation of their books. As you go through these examples, take note of how the authors use the book cover as a sales device. Take note of how the information is presented and how much information is presented.

For those of you who write books in series, consider creating an information page which provides guidance for readers. Here are some examples to look at:

https://www.eloisajames.com/faq/
https://juliaquinn.com/faq/
https://maryjoputney.com/frequently-asked-questions/
https://monicamccarty.com/faq.php?var=all

I realize all the examples above come from the romance genre. Romances tend to be written in series and, in my opinion, some of the best examples in terms of websites come from that genre. Some of the websites in the previous set of example websites also have key pages worth checking out for Series information.

Keep in mind that "Where do you get your inspiration/ideas?" and "When will the next book in X series be out?" is catnip to a voracious reader like me. You'll notice the examples from above are from multi-published authors with large backlists of books. They answer questions about themselves as well as their books. Since they all write in series, they use the "FAQ" page to answer questions about their series books—connecting characters, some background about time and place, etc.

Homework #2 – Start working on your pages for your books or your writing.

3) The next item on my list is to read some blog posts.

I've written an entire book on blogging. I started my presence in the on-line world as a blogger and still regularly blog. However, I am realistic about blogging and I also am aware there are only 24 hours in a day— some of which we should be sleeping.

If you are going to create blog posts, here are my thoughts:

1) The blog posts should be speaking to readers, not other writers.

2) The blog posts shouldn't be entirely focused on your next writing project; they should be a way to share yourself with your readers.

3) Accentuate the positives and hide the negatives. If you are only going to create blog posts every 6 months or so, see if you can remove the date from your blog posts so readers are not aware of how infrequently you blog. (This can be done on some platforms but not all.)

4) If you are going to blog, invite subscriptions (more on that in a future lesson) and use your blog posts to network with readers.

5) Google is attracted to new content. Regular blog posts are a great way to attract the attention of Google's search engine.

We'll touch on blogging and networking a bit more in this book;

however, if you are interested in learning more, I have a book focused on the subject of blogging for authors.

Homework #3 – Take a look at your blog if you have one. Read some of your more recent blog posts and refresh your memory as to the content. We'll come back to this content in a future lesson.

4) The last item on my list is a contact page/contact ideas.
I always suggest a form that readers can fill out if they are interested in reaching out. Using a form prevents your email address from being harvested from your website and allows you to respond in whatever fashion you want. Most website platforms allow for straightforward contact forms to be created.

Readers will also be interested in finding other places to interact with you. Can you be found on Facebook, Twitter, or Instagram? Can they join your mailing list?

Every platform will allow for the use of branded icons or submission forms to connect readers to all these places. Readers will instinctively recognize the blue Facebook "F" or the little bird for Twitter or the icon for Instagram. Make use of these tools to help your readers connect with you.

More on this information in a future lesson, but for today organize your thoughts and play with putting content on pages.

To summarize your homework for this lesson:
#1 – Look at the content on your About page and change if necessary or create from scratch if this content doesn't exist yet.
#2 – Start working on your Book/series page(s).

#3 – Read some of your blog posts to refresh your memory for a future lesson.

#4 – Create a contact form and put social media icons in place.

In the next lesson we are going to talk about organizing our menu structure to meet the needs of our readers—and we are going to talk about "User Experience."

LESSON 7 - USER EXPERIENCE AND MENU STRUCTURE

"UX" The latest catch phrase to hit the web-designing world. It stands for "User Experience." When putting together a website we tend to be of two different minds. The first is to be as helpful to our readers as possible. The second is to move our readers in the direction we want them to go.

Let's explore this. In a previous lesson, I talked about the experiment which was carried out with jars of jam. When people are given too many choices, they tend not to make a decision at all. The same exists on websites. The busier a website, the more choices that people have to make, the more likely they are to become overwhelmed and simply leave.

How do we apply this information?

On an author website, we primarily focus our attention to two different locations—the home page or the landing page and the menu line.

A little bit on the home page before we move on to the menu structure. We will circle back around to the landing page again in a future lesson. A landing page or home page is where readers arrive after they have typed your direct URL into a browser. If you remember back a few lessons, I said that people need to be able to identify they are in the right location pretty quickly. The time before they will leave will be measured in seconds.

I suggested that you make sure the section of your website that we consider "above the fold" clearly identifies you and what you write. If there is more than one author with the same name as you, clearly identify which one you are.

Beyond that, the main purpose of the landing page is to welcome readers and encourage them to explore further—and the implied purpose is to hope they look at your book(s) and buy a couple.

You don't want too much content on the landing page and you don't want too many choices as this will overwhelm readers and possibly send them away. (Unless they are as determined as I am, of course!)

The second target of "User Experience" is the menu line. We want to use the menu line to direct people in the direction we want them to go while not providing too much information all at once.

When readers come to our websites, we want them to:
1) Learn more about us
2) Learn more about and buy our books
3) Connect with us in other places (e.g., Facebook)
4) Join our mailing list/subscribe to our blog or both

There would be several other reasons for readers to seek information, such as finding local events they can attend, but we will start with the core reasons and branch out.

Because of what we want readers to do, we only provide the choices we want them to make. A menu line would have entries for:

- About
- Books
- Contact
- Blog

The labels can be anything you want them to be as long as they are crystal clear. Creativity is for your books, not for fancy words on your menu line. And if you don't blog, you wouldn't have that entry.

The pushback comes from how to list books when there is more than one. And the answer to that is we use the submenu structure. Our structure of the menu would then look something like this:

- About
- Books
  - Book 1
  - Book 2
- Contact
- Blog

If you have books in series, you might have something that looks like this:

- About
- Books
  - Series 1
    - Book 1
    - Book 2
  - Series 2
    - Book 1
    - Book 2
- Contact
- Blog

So, the question is how do we actually put this in place? It is a lot simpler than you might think. All the various platforms allow for a custom menu structure to be created. Locate the area on your site where the menu is controlled and specify each entry at both the primary, secondary and perhaps tertiary level.

Your homework today is to play with your menu structure to encourage readers to go in the direction you want them to go—and not overwhelm them.

LESSON 8 – THEMES – WHAT THEY ARE AND HOW TO CHOOSE ONE

In this lesson, we're going to talk about Themes. Almost without exception, all platforms used to create websites use themes. Some platforms use the term Theme and some use the term Template. These words mean the same thing.

So, what is a website theme? A theme is coding that controls the look and feel of your website. It controls the placement of content, the font used, the colors, the formatting, and so on.

There are likely thousands of themes just for WordPress alone. It seems that developers have created themes for every purpose.

Because the discussion of themes is better as a visual exercise, I'm going to send you off on a fact-finding mission! At some point in the development of a website, you need to choose a theme (or communicate to a developer what you want). Looking at a lot of choices helps to determine what you like and what you don't like.

Before we get to that point, let's review some of the words that we're going to use to refer to the parts and pieces of a website. These words are part of the Glossary, but I'll repeat them here.

Header - This is the section at the top of the website. It may be text, it may be pictures, it may be both.

Menu line - The menu line typically runs underneath the

header, although in some cases it is part of the header structure or above the header section. It contains clickable links to other pages or locations on your website.

Body - The body of the website spans the space between the header and footer. In some cases, it's divided into a number of smaller spaces.

Footer - The area at the bottom of the website.

Sidebar - The sidebar exists as a separate area of content in the body area of the website, usually to one side or another.

We're going to add one more word to our glossary for this lesson. That word is "balance." The human brain prefers balance. When it comes to websites, the brain is happier looking at content that has balance. What this means is that all parts and pieces of the website have roughly the same amount of information. They take up the same amount of room on the screen.

In the screenshot above, you see three columns of information from a section of a website. Although each one is a separate part, they all start and end at basically the same point on the computer screen.

Other examples would be: if you put a picture in place on the left-hand side of a page with text to the right, you want to make sure that the text ends at the bottom of the picture. The same thing with sidebars. You want to aim for the content in the sidebar to be the same length as the content in the rest of the body. It isn't always possible to achieve balance in a website, but it is something to strive for.

The other thing I'll point out here, and you can keep it in mind as you wander through some examples, is that people expect a certain format to exist. They will seek out what they feel is normal and you need to provide it. For example, only having a menu line in the footer would be disconcerting for some people. Visitors would have trouble finding it. We need to stick to norms as much as possible.

Below I've listed a selection of websites showcasing themes for most major platforms. Have a look through all the examples or just the ones appropriate to your platform. Most of the websites offer the ability to look at a demo version of themes. This will allow for viewing a sample as well as clicking on various links to see how the theme actually presents content.

As you go through the examples, jot down some notes. What do you like as well as what do you NOT like? What colors do you like? What layout presentation do you like?

WordPress.org themes:
    http://studiopress.com
    http://restored316.com
    http://9seeds.com
    https://wordpress.com/themes

WordPress.com themes:
    https://wordpress.com/themes

WIX themes:
    https://www.wix.com/website/templates

Weebly themes:
    https://www.weebly.com/ca/themes

. . .

Squarespace themes:

https://www.squarespace.com/templates/

As you can see from the examples presented in the above links. Most platforms will offer a selection of free themes or templates. Quite a few will offer premium themes—themes that come with a one-time or recurring cost. Many of the platforms will allow a custom theme to be created and put in place by a designer.

Regardless of what direction you go in, I always encourage looking at a wide variety of examples. See what you like; see what you don't like. See what is in fashion compared to what you currently have.

LESSON 9 - THE SCIENCE OF READING FOR WRITERS

This lesson has the title of "The Science of Reading for Writers." This is a subject that doesn't get a lot of traction in the author world but is a topic that needs to be covered in this book—primarily because what we know about reading with respect to websites goes against what most authors are taught about the craft of writing.

In my experience, authors try to put as much content on a website as they can. The landing page is full of paragraph after paragraph of dense information. Authors want people to scroll and scroll through detail after detail.

Sadly, readers of websites simply don't read that way. They scan, they keyword spot, they zigzag their way through content. Research on this has been going on for decades—this information is certainly not new. To help you understand some of the relevant research, I've created a 20-minute video for you to watch here: https://the-author-s-technical-help-desk.teachable.com/p/the-science-of-writing-for-readers

LESSON 10 - HOW TO CREATE CONTENT THAT IS CONNECTED, SCANNABLE, AND SHAREABLE

In this lesson we're going to talk about some of the specifics of content. This content can be on blog posts or on pages.

The three most important aspects of content are:

- Scannable
- Connected
- Shareable

As you learned in the video associated with the previous lesson, people consume content differently on an electronic device than they do in paper form. In other words, your website and your blog posts will be scanned, not read.

Many authors don't realize this and try to include as much information as possible to be as helpful as possible. The problem is, this doesn't match how readers will consume this type of information.

In this lesson we are going to talk about how to make your content "sticky" for your readers. To not only create content that they will consume, but also strategies to keep readers on your website. Studies show that the longer readers stay on your site, the more likely they are to make a buying decision.

Let's start with the idea of your content being **Scannable**.

We talked about this behavior on the video. People, when reading on electronic sources, don't actually read left to right, top to bottom. They scan, they zigzag, they keyword spot.

And yes, we pander to this behavior!

We create short paragraphs which have white space, blocks of graphics, headers, subheads, quotes, numbered lists, lines of bold or italic text. We use these devices to catch their attention—to keep them reading.

Let's apply this information to something like a book details page. In previous lessons I have encouraged you to have a cover graphic and blurb and purchase or buy links. I also encouraged you to include what we call "social proof" in the form of review quotes from readers or reviewers. I also encouraged you to include an excerpt so that readers can give your writing style a "test drive." Present the information in sections.

https://lynnrayeharris.com/books/hot-seal/

Website Tips & Tricks

https://www.jillshalvis.com/lost-and-found-sisters

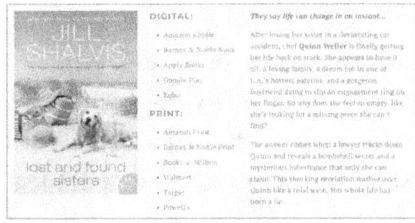

The two above examples show different presentations of content on a book details page. Just as an aside, you'll notice that they are both balanced, but in different ways.

Is there a "right" answer for the creation of a book details page? Not really. There may be a "right" answer for you, but not one generally. I encourage you to look at examples and test out samples. There are a lot of examples I look at that I feel cross the line from being helpful to being overwhelming, but as we'll learn a few lessons from now, using our stats we can "watch" what our visitors do and see how they respond to our content.

The examples above are examples of book details pages, but

"scannability" can be seen on blog posts also. I'll encourage you to visit a few of my favorite marketing blogs to see examples of "scannability." Take a few moments and have a look at Neil Patel's blog at http://neilpatel.com and Copyblogger at http://CopyBlogger.com.

The next topic we are going to address is **Connected**. What I mean by connected is putting hyperlinks or other devices on our website/blog posts to give our readers something to click or tap on.

There are a number of advantages of doing this. The first and most important reason is the longer we keep readers on our websites, the more likely they are to do something we want them to do—buy a book, join a mailing list, etc.

However, when readers are presented with a great big mass of information, they are more likely to become overwhelmed and leave. Remember the survey I talked about with the jars of jam—when presented with too many choices people tend to make no choice at all.

When we talk about the word *connected*, we are talking about using hyperlinks to connect one piece of content on your website with another piece of content. I've included a screenshot below from Rachel Thompson's author website. The red underlined text is text that is hyperlinked.

Although I don't feel that there is any "perfect" example, I do feel that using hyperlinks to connect readers to Amazon buy pages or other pages of one's website is necessary. It connects your content to other content or other relevant websites. I encourage you to visit a few of your favorite authors' websites and see if they have attempted to connect their content in a way that is helpful to you as a reader or visitor to their site.

The idea of connectedness can also exist on blog posts in a number of ways. You can use hyperlinks in a blog post to link to similar content that you have mentioned or written about previously. You can also make use of an automatic functionality to allow your readers to be aware of other similar content.

In the screenshot below is an example of "Related Posts." This is a common WordPress plugin that is put in place to display at the bottom of blog posts, either as a standalone plugin or as part of the Jetpack functionality

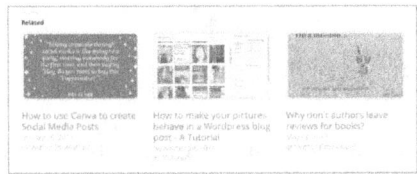

WIX, Weebly, etc. all have similar functionalities that can be used as well. Look among the choices your platform offers for this type of functionality and consider adding it to your website.

Connectedness doesn't need to be limited to posts or pages within your own website. Consider hyperlinking to influencers in your niche. This will catch attention in a positive way!

Lastly, on the subject of connectedness, consider creating a

feature on your website which connects to all your fellow authors. Google likes this sort of thing.

The last subject for this lesson is **Sharable**.

We need to create content that our readers want to share with their friends. Just like when we get to the end of a really good book, we reach out to someone we know would like this book and let them know. The same is true for our websites. Whether it be for the content on our website or blog posts, we need to make it easy for our readers to share it with their friends. And, we need to remember to ask our readers to share.

The most efficient way of having our readers share our content with their friends is to use share buttons or icons. In the screenshot below you can see one example of this.

I'm sure you have seen similar buttons on websites—perhaps on your website. If clicked on, the share button allows a reader to share information on **their** social media accounts (not yours). Because it isn't dependent on what social media accounts you have, you need to include as many choices as you can.

Many readers have sizable social media platforms. Sharing with my thousands of Twitter followers is much more powerful than just leaving a comment on a post.

Some of the information we have covered in this lesson can seem overwhelming. However, if this is attacked a little bit at a time, it is less intimidating.

As we come to the end of this lesson, I encourage you to complete the homework below before moving on.

Homework #1 - Look at the information you have created for your "About" page and Book(s) page. See if it is Scannable. Is it connected or hyperlinked to other content if appropriate?

Homework #2 - See if you can put functionality—like Related Posts—in place to help automatically suggest more content for your readers to read (if you have a blog). Although I use a plugin to do this on WordPress, the functionality is available on most platforms. Most platforms will have help documents to assist you in putting this in place.

Homework #3 - See if you can put share buttons at the bottom of all your content. Again, I use plugins on WordPress sites, but all the platforms I am familiar with will offer this sort of functionality. They may call it a gadget, or an app, but don't hesitate to use the help documents to guide you towards the right choice for your site.

LESSON 11 - HOW TO WRANGLE PICTURES

This lesson is going to be all about pictures. If you remember back to one of the beginning lessons, I had you test the page loading speed of your website. At the time I mentioned that pictures or graphics can be problematic for websites. Pictures can take up a lot of space and pictures can interfere with loading speed.

The average hosting account allows for about 10 GB of storage space. That's for WordPress.org; WordPress.com isn't as generous. The free WordPress.com account allows for 3 GB of storage. It is possible to purchase more storage. Other platforms' hosting accounts vary in size as well; however, they do have a limit.

While 10 GB may seem like a lot of space, my iPhone actually has 32 GB of space, so 10GB is not that generous.

In my experience, most authors run into problems with too many pictures on their website—especially if they have an active blog. The primary reason for this is because authors are using high-resolution pictures when they're really not necessary. Many of the authors I work with don't understand how to size pictures and, because of this, they just use pictures in whatever size they obtain them in.

The first thing that we're going to talk about in this lesson is how to change the size and the resolution of a picture.

How you do that can depend on the computer you are using.

I have a Mac so let's start there. The most straightforward way to wrangle pictures on a Mac is to open them with Preview (a program that comes with all Macs). Click on Tools and then Adjust Size and you will see a view similar to the screenshot below:

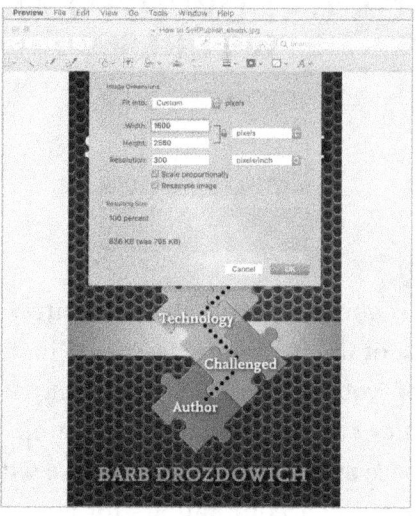

In the screenshot above, you can see one of my book covers. The height is 2560 px, the width is 1600px and the resolution is 300 dpi. This is a great size and resolution for a cover graphic—it fits Amazon's requirements perfectly—but is overkill for a website.

In the screenshot below, I show my website with some numbers annotated.

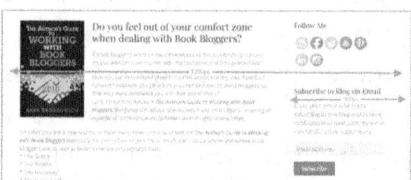

The width of an average website is typically around 1200px and the sidebar area is typically about 300px. So...if the sidebar is about 300px, compare that to the size of the book cover in the graphic above. It might be 150 or 175px. Compare that to the existing width of a typical cover graphic which is about 1500 or 1600px wide.

As you can see with the numbers in the above graphic, if I reduce the width of the graphic by half, it reduces the size by more than half. The full-size graphic is 803 KB and the smaller one is 322KB.

What's that saying? Every little bit helps. What seems like a lot of space when you first start can easily be filled up with larger pictures than you will ever actually need on your website.

I encourage you to reduce the size of the pictures you use on your website before you upload them to your site.

As you are changing the size of graphics, it's a great idea to give each picture a functional name. Frequently we get cover graphics (for example) from our graphic artists that have the title of "BD-HTSPaB-Full" or whatever fits with their typical naming convention. If I change the title of this picture to "How-to-self-publish-a-book-Barb-Drozdowich" when Google reads this picture it sees information that is more helpful!

If you are running a PC there are a lot of programs that can be used for your computer to wrangle pictures. Instead of adding another program, I tend to send folks to http://befunky.com

As you can see in the screenshot above, a picture can be uploaded and then either reduced in size using the absolute size (rectangle) or by reducing by percentages (arrow).

Whichever method you use, make sure you don't overload your website with unnecessarily large pictures.

Alt Text

The "Alt text" field is a description field for pictures or graphics. It is considered to be essential not only for Search Engine Optimization, but also to serve as a description for a picture.

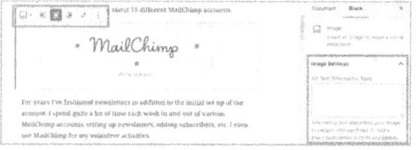

To find this area on WordPress (either .org or .com) click on the picture once (in the edit version of either a page or a post) and your screen will resemble the screenshot above.

The box to the right has the label of "Image Settings" and the first item is "Alt Text." Look at the description below the blank box. It reads "Alternative text describes your image to people who can't see it. Add a short description with its key details." There are a lot of people who are visually challenged and use what's called a "screen reader" to "view" a website. The screen reader will read a website's content to them. Typically, graphics or pictures can't be "seen" but text about them can be read. Use this field to describe the picture/graphic to these folks.

The alt text field exists on all other platforms as well as Word-

Press. Just click on the picture and information can be added about that picture—one of which is the alt text.

When you enter information in the alt text box, not only are you helping people who use a screen reader, but you are also adding information to Google. You are telling Google what this picture is. Be self-serving! If the graphic is of a book cover, list the title and your name and describe your genre at a bare minimum. The cover graphic I showed previously of one of my books would have the alt text of "How to Self-Publish a Book: For the Technology Challenged Author by Author and Technical trainer Barb Drozdowich - a great guide to self-publishing a book in today's publishing world."

Once I get to this point in the explanation, I get authors saying something like "You don't expect me to go back and add an alt text to every picture on my website, do you??" The answer is no, especially if you have a lot of content on your website. I do encourage you to enter an alt text for all your book covers at a bare minimum. Then you can enter this information for every picture going forward.

How to make pictures behave.

The last subject we will talk about today is how to make pictures do what you want them to do. Some of this will be covered in screenshots, but I also have YouTube videos that I will point you to at the end of this lesson.

Pictures are much happier if given specific instructions. They WANT to be told where they are supposed to be.

In WordPress.org and WordPress.com if a picture is clicked on when in the edit view, a little menu appears at the top as you can see in the screenshot above. There are three buttons that allow for the picture placement—left justified, centered, and right justified. Right now, WordPress tends to automatically left-justify any picture that is uploaded. Other platforms have different defaults. Regardless of where a picture starts out, make sure it has specific instructions. Don't let it decide.

The screenshot above is for WordPress, but a similar situation exists for most platforms. If a picture is clicked on, the picture design elements can be controlled and more information can be added to that picture—from captions, to alt text to hyperlinks. Experiment with the platform you use and see what it will allow you to add/adjust with pictures.

No specific homework for this lesson other than encouraging you to experiment with some pictures! I have a YouTube video that focuses on the picture functionality on WordPress that will help those of you using WordPress. The Video can be found here: https://www.youtube.com/watch?v=XVHqYd8tFXU

LESSON 12 – HOW TO "SEE" YOUR AUDIENCE

In this lesson we're going to learn all about audiences. How to figure out who is visiting your website. What facts you should care about and what facts you can ignore.

We're going to talk about two commonly used applications/services to learn about your audience—Jetpack Stats and Google Analytics. If you have a WordPress.com site, you automatically have Jetpack Stats. If you have a WordPress.org site, you will need to put Jetpack in place. It typically isn't automatically added. If you have a WIX, Weebly, Squarespace or a website builder site, you don't have access to Jetpack and will be only using Google Analytics.

Google Analytics is a more widely used service than Jetpack Stats and is available to be used by any type of website. The only exception is a WordPress.com site with one of the lower packages. Google Analytics is allowed with the business package, however.

There are a ton of different applications or services or plugins available to measure your audience. They aren't all great tools. Some of these types of applications measure anything that comes to your website—real people, Google bots, spam trolls—everyone and everything. Why a service would want to measure non-real visitors is beyond me. Don't get me started on THAT discussion!

In fact, there is no perfect application for determining the characteristics of our visitors. They all get it wrong occasionally. Because of this, I encourage you to take all the numbers we'll talk about with a grain of salt. Look at generalities; look at increases and decreases. Don't obsess over one number here or there.

So...what should you care about?

You should be interested in where your audience is arriving from. What caused them to visit your website? You should be interested in what people are paying attention to on your website. What are the popular pages (and posts if you have a blog)? What are people clicking on? And if you have access to Google Analytics, it's interesting to find out where your audience is from and what type of device they are viewing your website on. Another interesting piece of information is: How long do visitors to your website stay and do they leave quickly?

Do I care how many overall visitors you have to your website? Nope...not really. The main reason for this—the number of visitors is what most people tend to obsess over. Checking multiple times a day to see if there has been another visitor. That's not helpful to an author's mental state!

So ... I advocate paying attention to things you can control and things that are interesting. Information you can take action on.

We're going to talk about what all these things are that we should be paying attention to and then look at screenshots of where this information can be found both on Jetpack Stats as well as Google Analytics.

Referrers – is the referring source of traffic to your website. It may be Facebook or Twitter, it may be another author's website, it may be a blogger's website. We want to keep track of friends and we want to know if actions on social media are sending visitors to our website.

Top Posts & Pages – is the list of the top (usually) 10 blog posts or pages that visitors are viewing.

Clicks – the section which lets you know what visitors to your website click on.

Location – where your visitors are located geographically. This may not be where you think.

Technology – what device(s) your visitors are using to view your website.

Time on site – from start to finish, how long, on average, your visitors are staying on your website. The longer the better!

In this next section, I'll share some screenshots that explain where to find each piece of information.

We'll start the screenshots with Jetpack Stats and screenshots from a WordPress.com account. There are slight differences between what is seen on WordPress.com and WordPress.org sites, as I'll explain below.

To find this information, look for the display on the dashboard.

This initial view shows a bar graph of visitors for each day for a month. It can be adjusted to show this information by month or year also. There are summaries at the bottom of the graph.

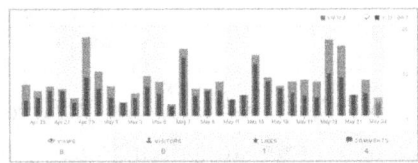

Scrolling down below this area, you'll be able to see the Post & Pages section, Search terms (which we ignore) and Countries. WordPress.com allows you to initially see about 7 or 8 top posts and pages. If you click on the sideways arrow you can see (and I suggest) a larger block of time —7 days, 30 days, etc. Numbers are always more meaningful when looked at over a longer period of time.

The box labeled Countries, will give you a snapshot of where your visitors are from—again, click on the sideways arrow to see a variety of time periods. (This information is typically not available on the version of Jetpack for .org accounts.)

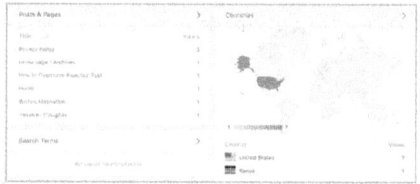

The next section (see below) to direct your attention to is "Clicks." This lists items on your site that people have clicked on—such as buy links for your books or clicks on your social media icons.

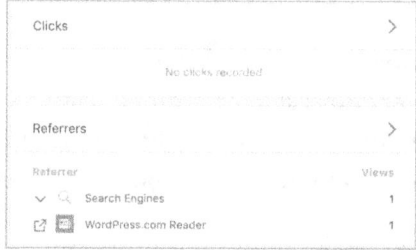

The section below Clicks is Referrers. Referrers is the section which will list where visitors start their journey to find you. This may be a Search Engine such as Google, it may be Facebook or it may be another blog or website. As above, click on the sideways arrow to see a larger selection of results.

Because there are small differences between .com and .org versions of Jetpack, find below screenshots from .org.

As you can see below, the top section of the display shows not only a bar graph but some interesting totals, such as "Best ever" and numbers from the life of the website—interesting, but not something we use.

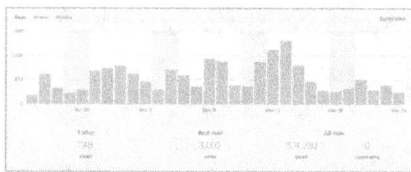

Scroll down below the bar graphic and you'll see the section in the screenshot below—made up of Referrers, Search Engine Terms and Top Posts & Pages.

As with the description for the .com version, Referrers tells you where your traffic is coming from—great for identifying the effectiveness of a Facebook promotion for example. Search Engine Terms can be entertaining, but Google no longer allows us much information about the search terms people use when searching for us. Because of this, I generally suggest ignoring this section.

To the right in the above screenshot is a selection of Top Posts & Pages. As described previously, this is a list of the top content your visitors are interested in. By clicking on Summaries, you can see a bigger selection of results.

Scroll further down and you'll see the section depicted in the screenshot below:

Clicks will let you know what people are clicking on. This will give you an idea of some of the actions your visitors are taking during their time on your site.

Moving on to the topic of **Google Analytics**. Regardless of how you attach your site to Google Analytics, the full array of results can be overwhelming. I suggest using a plugin on WordPress.org to connect the website with Google Analytics or making use of the various apps offered on other platforms. There are a wide variety of plugins/apps available for this purpose. WIX and Weebly will allow for connection with Google Analytics via code placement and SquareSpace has built-in analytics. Please also find below references for other types of platforms at the end of this chapter.

Before we go on to the description, keep in mind that with a little elbow grease, any website can be hooked up to a Google Analytics account and the information described in the above sections can also be viewed via Google Analytics. I generally don't like that section of the display when I can rely on Jetpack stats; hence, my preferences.

I like allowing a small snapshot of information to exist on the dashboard of a website for a number of reasons. The most important reason is it is less overwhelming. By focusing attention on a small number of items, the information can be meaningful rather than intimidating. Not all platforms will allow this sort of display, but if yours does, I encourage you to take advantage of it.

The starting point of the Google Analytics display is typically similar to the screenshot below. The two labels show "Last 30 Days" and "Sessions." This information will show the visitors for the last 30 days (and that time period can be changed). At the bottom of the display is "Session Duration" which indicates the average time people spend on the website. Another interesting piece of information is "Bounce Rate." This indicates how fast people leave the site. The higher the number, the quicker people leave.

Website Tips & Tricks

If the "Sessions" menu is changed to "Location" as seen in the screenshot below, you can view a graphic display as well as a list of where visitors are geographically located when they visit a website. The information and numbers may surprise you.

If that drop down is changed again—to "Technology" you will

be able to see the type of device people use when viewing a website. Again, this information may not be what you expected.

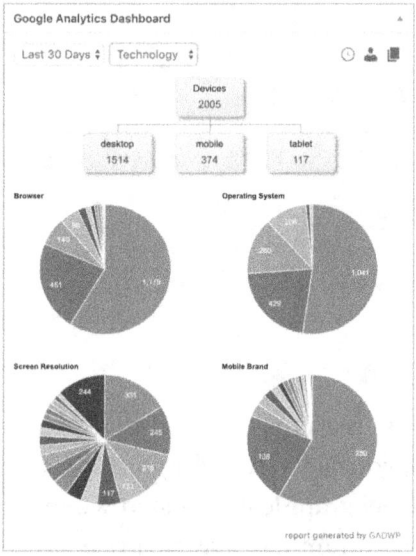

So...why all this information, beyond the idea that "Knowledge is power"? Several fold, really. As authors, we want people to buy our books. If we go back to the first few lessons, you'll remember that Google doesn't sell books—Amazon et al. do. But visitors to your website hopefully sign up to your mailing list, subscribe to your blog, click on links to find you on social media, and click on links to purchase your books. By studying the actions of the audience, or visitors to our site, we can determine if any of this is being achieved.

As with many things, we need to "read the tea leaves" to see if our efforts are paying off. For example, if you have 100 people visiting your website and no one is clicking on the Facebook icon to follow you on Facebook, perhaps it isn't visible enough. If those hundred people visit your book details pages and not one clicks on a buy link to purchase a copy at Amazon, etc., perhaps look at the layout of that page and see if the buy links aren't obvious enough. See if the blurb isn't compelling enough.

And if your audience is primarily from India and the Far East—as is true of one of my sites—there is not a lot of point offering a US only giveaway, as that will just annoy your readers.

Again, knowledge is power! I hope you enjoyed this lesson. Your only homework is to pick around at your numbers and see if you can learn more about your audience.

References:
Godaddy site builder:
https://ca.godaddy.com/help/add-google-analytics-8433
WIX:
https://support.wix.com/en/article/adding-your-google-analytics-tracking-id-to-your-wix-site
Weebly:
https://www.weebly.com/blog/getting-started-with-google-analytics/
SquareSpace:
https://support.squarespace.com/hc/en-us/articles/205815608-Using-Google-Analytics-with-Squarespace

LESSON 13 - SAFETY & SECURITY

In this lesson we're going to look at a few general topics and a few platform-specific topics and our overarching theme will be safety and security.

The first topic we will discuss in this lesson is the subject of backups. Do you have a backup of your site? Is there an automated backup process in place right now? Is it something you set up or are you relying on your hosting company to take care of your site?

Let's discuss, starting with WordPress. Regardless of which version of WordPress you are using, you can take what's known as an "export" of your site. Log onto your site, go to Tools, and choose Export. (On WordPress.com you need to click on WP Admin and then Tools and then Export. Once you choose Export you will choose the free version of an export.) With both versions of WordPress, you choose "All Content" and then click on "Download Export File." This will give you what's known as an XML file. This contains all the content of your site—not fancy and doesn't include the design elements, but your posts, pages and media (pictures) will be contained in this file.

. . .

If you are using a different platform here are your instructions:

WIX: https://support.wix.com/en/article/request-creating-a-backup-of-your-site
Weebly: https://www.weebly.com/app/help/us/en/topics/back-up-your-site
SquareSpace: https://support.squarespace.com/hc/en-us/articles/206566687
GoDaddy Web builder: https://ca.godaddy.com/help/backing-up-or-restoring-your-website-2992

Before we go any further, go take an export of your site and decide on a spot you can safely store it. Perhaps on your computer, perhaps on a zip drive, perhaps in cloud storage like Dropbox.

Many of the hosting companies will take care of automatic backups of websites. Whether the website is WordPress, Wix, Weebly or some other platform, most have an automatic backup process in place. In fact, that is a selling feature of many hosting companies.

Where the problems start to occur is when the hosting company goes out of business, or when the invoice for hosting isn't paid, that backup may be gone. In fact, it is possible for WordPress.com (among others) to shut down a site for infringement of rules. If the hosting site is solely in charge of backups and the site is shut down, typically the backups are gone also. (Not to fear monger—this doesn't frequently happen, but it has on occasion.) For these reasons I like to encourage website owners to have at a bare minimum an export file in their control. Too many phone calls involving tears for me not to encourage this action!

The only platform which allows for independent (user controlled) scheduled backups is WordPress.org. To accomplish this, I typically encourage the use of a plugin. There are many choices for this function, as well as positives and negatives for each. My preference is a plugin that creates and stores a backup in a location other than the hosting account. My plugin of choice is UpDraft Plus and I store backups in my Dropbox account. This plugin allows me to schedule backups to occur at whatever frequency I choose, and it chugs along automatically. I don't have to babysit this—it just happens.

Why automation and why store the backup in a different location than the hosting company? Automation removes the human element from the equation. Back before I moved to using plugins that have a scheduling function, I religiously backed up all my sites every Saturday morning after breakfast. I had a reminder on my calendar and I rarely forgot. Having this process automatically occur simplifies my life! For those of you who have sites on WordPress.com, WIX, Weebly, SquareSpace or a website builder, independent automated backups are not possible. I encourage you to periodically download and safely store an export of your site—especially if you are blogging and adding new content on a regular basis.

Why do I suggest not storing the backup on your hosting account? The simple answer is that it takes up room. If you remember back a few lessons ago I mentioned that hosting companies have space or storage limits. By storing backup files on the hosting account, you are needlessly taking up space that could be used for the website itself. This isn't a concern for a new or smaller site but is most definitely a concern for an established site which has an active blog.

Let's move on to security. A common comment I hear from authors is some version of "my site won't be hacked because I'm not famous." That statement couldn't be more wrong. Hacking is rarely a targeted crime—it is a crime of opportunity. Yes, big news item hacks like Sony, Equifax, Target, Yahoo, etc. are targeted, but those are few and far between. I like to compare hacking to leaving your car door unlocked and assuming no one will open it and steal the loose change from your dash or leaving your front door unlocked and assume no one will check and see if there is anything to steal.

I can't count the number of sites I have dealt with that have been hacked.

The screenshot above is one example of what can happen.

So why do hackers access websites? Other than destruction of reputation, websites of non-famous people/businesses can be used as a hub for the hackers to send out phishing emails or attacks on other sites. Or as you can see above, simply redirecting a site to sell Viagra. Regardless of what happens, we want to take steps to prevent this from happening.

Step #1 - Log in passwords. A log in password should be reasonably complicated. As I'm sure you've read elsewhere, it should NOT be ABCDE and it shouldn't be your first name or the name of your first book or the name of your cat. It should be a combination of small letters, capital letters, numbers and symbols—and use the symbols that people don't typically use like ^, >, + or } As a hint, I suggest people create a password with the symbols first and letters/numbers last. For websites that have requirements for a certain "strength" of a password, this is easier to achieve using this method.

Also, as I'm sure you've read elsewhere, your password should be different for every site. I understand that this is difficult to achieve in real life. I am responsible for hundreds of login credentials and I use a password management program on my computer. Because of this program, one click and login credentials are entered for every site I have access to. This program works across my desktop and laptop computers, tablet and phone. Worth the small investment as it makes the wrangling of passwords so much more straightforward.

Step #2 - Updates. All platforms have software that is updated periodically. These updates are sometimes functional, allowing increased or improved functionality to be introduced. Sometimes these updates are in response to a known security threat. Some platforms have updates that are user controlled; others have updates that are out of the user's hands entirely. The updates which are out of the user's hands can mostly be ignored. If a notification comes through, perhaps having a look at the public side of your website is a good idea to ensure that nothing is amiss. This rarely happens, but it's a good idea to check.

Plugins and Updates - What are they? Why should we have them? Plugins exist only on WordPress.org websites and the upper package of WordPress.com websites. These are bits of code which are put in place to perform a specific function. This function maybe be an internal function, such as AKISMET which isolates spam comments, or it may be an external function, such as a Mailing list signup form that is embedded in a page or the sidebar of a website.

Thinking about these examples, you'll realize that most platforms have a wide variety of such additions of function. They may call them widgets, gadgets or apps, but WordPress.org is the only platform that has plugins which need updating by the user of the website.

Let's stay with the subject of plugins and talk about not only security but also updates. Plugins are regularly updated by their developers in response to a need to add functionality or in response to a security threat. If an update is available for a plugin, a number in a circle appears on the website dashboard menu like the screenshot below:

This update is also indicated on the actual plugin entry. If you click on Plugins and Installed Plugins, you'll notice that the entry has a link that's labeled "update now." Click on that link and the update proceeds all by itself. Whether the update is for security reasons or simply to update or improve functions, if a plugin indicates it has an update, it should be updated relatively promptly.

Hackers are criminals of opportunity. They take advantages of security weaknesses to gain entry into a website. An out of date plugin is therefore, by definition, a security risk.

Plugins that have been abandoned by their developers are also a potential security threat. I suggest that all plugins are checked every 6 or 8 months to make sure they are being kept up to date—and if not, they should be replaced.

To check to see if a plugin is being kept up to date, click on Plugins and then Installed Plugins and then you'll notice each record has a link labeled "View Details." Click on that link and you'll see something similar to the screenshot below:

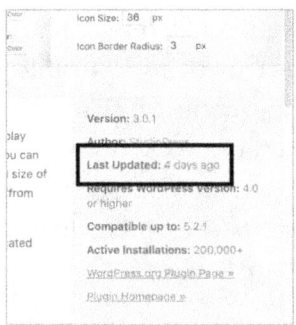

The area you are interested in is when it was last updated. The example above indicates the plugin was updated 4 days ago. If this field says a year or more, likely the plugin has been abandoned.

Let's talk about plugins in another way. As I said previously, plugins are bits of code that add functionality to your site. It can be a lot of geeky fun to see what cool things can be added to a website using fancy plugins. However, every time a website loads by a browser program, all the plugins have to load also. As a result, too many plugins aren't necessarily a good thing. I generally suggest that the number of plugins be in the 8 to 12 range. If you have more than that—and if your website loads a bit slowly—have a look at what you have on your site and decide if you need all those plugins. Perhaps getting rid of some unnecessary plugins will speed up the loading of your website.

. . .

One last quick note before we end this lesson since we have been talking about updates. Not only does the technology involved in a website need to be kept up to date, so does the content. Too many authors think that a website is a "one and done" kind of thing. They can create it and then ignore it. This couldn't be further from the truth. You should be continually updating information—adding new books, making sure the buy links are accurate when you move books from KDP Select to being available everywhere, etc. You should also get into the habit of giving the public side of your website a once over every week or so. Set yourself a memory minder—an event on your Google calendar perhaps —and have a look at what your readers see when they visit. There is nothing more embarrassing than having a reader point out an issue to you....

What's your homework for this lesson? It's fairly straightforward. Make sure your login password is somewhat complicated and if you are overwhelmed by the wrangling of passwords, look at using a password program on your computer. The one I use is 1Password, but there are others.

If you have a WordPress.org site, look at your plugins and see if they are all up to date, not abandoned, and necessary. Perhaps set yourself up a method of remembering to check the public side of your website every so often.

LESSON 14 - FOLLOWERS, SUBSCRIBERS, ETC.

In this lesson we're going to talk about a series of networking actions. In my experience, authors who work in the corporate world totally get the concept of networking. Authors who wrangle a bunch of children and have navigated the world of swim lessons, piano lessons and dance also understand the world of networking. At its base, networking is just chatting with other people and learning information. In the old-fashioned world, it is adding cards to your Rolodex.

In the website world, networking also exists, but since it takes a different form, many of the authors I work with need a bit of guidance to get them on the right path. In the website world, at its base, networking is letting people know the various "places" you can be found, encouraging them to find you or follow you there, and then communicating with them.

Ultimately books are sold by word of mouth. We sometimes lose sight of that fact. We find out about books from a trusted source. In today's world that trusted source might be the author via a newsletter or a blog post, it might be from a favorite blogger, it might be a favorite newsletter like BookBub. I'm sure we've all suggested a favorite book to someone. It's what readers do!

. . .

Back to the subject of websites. We need to make sure we let visitors to our websites know everywhere we can be found. But remember, hide the negatives and accentuate the positives.

Let's start with **social media**. We want to let our readers know where else we are active other than the website. You'll notice I said "active." If you aren't active on a particular social media, don't emphasize that!

How can you share information about social media? This can be done several ways:

1) Follow buttons or icons
2) Embedded stream widgets

1) Follow buttons or icons look like this:

Each social media's icon is included in the set and connected to YOUR account on that social media. Usually the block of icons has a title like "Follow Me" or "Find Me Here" or something similar. It is possible to place each social media in individual widgets or gadgets or apps (depending on your platform) but I suggest putting everything together in one block. It's less confusing for readers and takes up less valuable real estate that can better be used for advertising your books. As a quick plug for the new version of WordPress, did you realize that icons like this can be placed at the end of a blog post now?

2) Embedded stream widgets look like this:

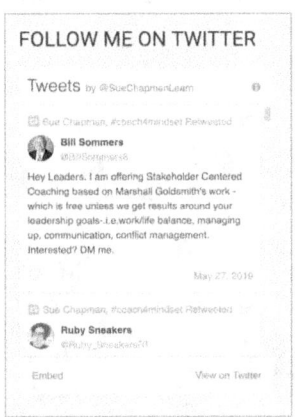

All the platforms allow for, at a bare minimum, the embedding of a Facebook stream widget/app and Twitter stream widget/app. Several of the platforms allow for more choices than just that.

Why would you share this kind of information? If you are particularly active or interactive on a social media, advertising that fact using a stream widget will encourage enthusiasm from your readers and encourage them to join you.

However, hide the negatives. If you aren't active, don't use this type of function as it just makes your inactivity glaringly obvious.

Let's move on to **subscribers.** Most website platforms allow for 3 types of subscribers:

1) RSS subscribers

2) Blog subscribers
3) Mailing list subscribers

1) RSS subscribers

RSS stands for "Really Simple Syndication." Subscribing to a website's RSS is also called "Subscribing to a feed." The icon that represents this is:

It is typically orange and is often mistaken for a WIFI symbol by those who are unfamiliar with this function. Readers use a program called a "Feed Reader" such as "Feedly" to subscribe to a website's feed. It is seen by some to be old-fashioned, but in fact, is still quite common. Most websites innately have a RSS feed and the address is http://yourdomian.cm/feed/ By putting the RSS icon in place, you are encouraging folks to add your website to their selection of websites they keep track of. This is more commonly done for blogs than websites, as the RSS feed will share new content. A website that is mostly static doesn't have much to share.

Technical note: People who make use of a feed reader program such as "Feedly" to keep track of websites don't need instructions. Generally speaking, they know what they are doing, but putting a

RSS icon in place reminds them that they can "subscribe to your feed."

2) Blog subscriptions

There are many different ways to allow/encourage blog subscription. And it should go without mentioning that this function is specific to blogs. My favorite comes from the Jetpack set of functionalities and on my website it looks like this:

This functionality allows interested readers to enter their email address (and perhaps their name). Every time a new blog post is published, they will get an email notification letting them know this.

There are quite a few different ways of putting this functionality in place, but regardless of which method you choose, think about a few things:

1) Is it obvious what you are asking people to sign up for?
2) Is it clear what information you want them to supply?
3) Are you setting the expectations correctly?
4) Are you hiding the negatives and accentuating the positives?

. . .

Let's talk about each one of these points. The first two points from above are somewhat connected. Be clear about what you are asking people to enter their email address for. In this case we are asking folks to subscribe to a blog. Make sure the wording says that.

Make sure that people are aware of what they are getting. As you can see in the screenshot above: "Enter your email address to subscribe to this blog and receive notifications of new posts by email." I could add information about the estimated frequency of the blog posts to add more clarity. In terms of hiding the negatives, I have included a line that lets people know how many subscribers are present. If I only had 4 subscribers, I wouldn't do that, but since the number is larger, I share that information. People have a fear of missing out. By showing how many people have subscribed, many will join an obviously popular group.

3) Mailing Lists

Let's move on to the topic of Mailing Lists. A Mailing List is a group of email addresses (and sometimes more information) which is held by an Email Marketing Service like MailChimp or MailerLite. The information is typically collected using a widget/gadget/app on your website and the information is transferred automatically to the service you have chosen.

A simple example is seen below:

Subscribe to my mailing list

* indicates required

Email Address *

SUBSCRIBE

The screenshot above is what the default signup form looks like from MailChimp. All of the services have a default signup form that looks similar to this. It has a simple title and has one or more fields to collect information and a button that can be clicked on that says "Subscribe" or "Sign-up" or something similar.

Let's go back to the suggestions for blog subscription forms and apply them to this type of signup:
    1) Is it obvious what you are asking people to sign up for?
    2) Is it clear what information you want them to supply?
    3) Are you setting the expectations correctly?
    4) Are you hiding the negatives and accentuating the positives?

In the mailing list screenshot, is it obvious what people are signing up for? Basically, yes. They are joining a mailing list. Most people these days understand what a mailing list is. Is it clear what information you want? Again, yes. The field to enter the email address is clearly labeled.

Are you setting expectations? Nope. You are simply asking readers to enter their email address to join a list. You haven't indicated what kind of information they will receive from you. You haven't indicated what the frequency will be of this information.

Study after study indicates if expectations are set, people are happier. If you tell people you will send out one newsletter each quarter and you email them every second day, readers will be annoyed and leave your list. If you want to email every second day, let people know you are going to do that, and they can decide if that's what they want.

I've set up my mailing list subscription to be a two-part process. I have a graphic on my website as follows:

When the red button is clicked on, the following form appears:

When a first name and email address are entered and the "Sign Up" button is clicked, they receive a confirmation note and if they follow through, they are added to my merry group.

My instructions or process is clearer than the first example. Could it be clearer? I'm sure it could be. In fact, I typically tweak this process every so often to try to increase the clarity.

One last note about this process. If you send all new subscribers a "Welcome" type of note which reiterates what they have joined and how often you will be communicating with them, these new folks are much more likely to be happy members of your group.

How do we actually set up a signup form on our websites? Generally speaking, every major email marketing service will connect with all the common website platforms in a relatively seamless way. Some of the website builder programs are not as straightforward, but every one of them will allow for code to be added, resulting in the display of a signup form. Most of the email marketing services provide detailed instructions to help. Wordpress.org offers a wide selection of plugins to help with this connection process.

Which service do you choose for your Mailing List and Newsletters? For the most part, that is personal preference. I used to send all my beginners to MailChimp because they had a relatively straightforward program and allowed for 2000 email addresses to be added before they started charging a fee. Over the past 2 years or so, their program has gotten more and more complicated resulting in frustration from many beginners. I've even been known to swear at the computer on occasion. I now send beginners to MailerLite. It is a simpler program to use but only allows for 1000 free additions to the list.

Are there other choices? Yes! I personally use Campaign Monitor, and have several authors who use Active Campaign, ConvertKit and Constant Contact. All have positives and negatives.

In terms of homework, I encourage you to look at your networking efforts and see if you can improve the clarity, improve the visibility, or add some features that aren't currently in place.

LESSON 15 - DEVELOP A PLAN GOING FORWARD

Too many authors create—or have created for them—a website and then they cross it off the "To-Do" list and move on with their writing.

Websites these days are not a "one and done" kind of thing. They require attention on a number of levels.

I'm not sure if websites were ever intended to be a one-time creation. Perhaps, in their infancy websites were considered more static than changeable, regardless, this is simply no longer the case.

Not only does the state of your career change—you release new books, you put books on sale and so on—but the state of security in today's world is also changing. Bad actors are constantly trying to gain access to places that they shouldn't be.

Because of all of this, we are going to make a plan for maintaining your website going forward.

. . .

Content

The website for an author who is continually creating new books and releasing them to the world needs this information added to their website. In fact, for a website that is visited by readers, adding information about "coming soon" books is an advantage.

I suggest setting a calendar reminder (I love Google Calendar for this) for every 6 months. Block out an hour of time on that day and review all the content on your website. Is anything out of date? Click on everything. Are there broken links? Did you put your books in KDP Select and need to change your buy links? And perhaps take a few minutes and look at your stats. Are people making use of your social media links? Are folks signing up for your website blog? Are they clicking on your buy links? If the answer is no, or not really, are there changes you can make? Can you change the wording? Can you change the colors? Can you change the size or positioning? If it might be helpful, get a fellow author to have a look. If you have a responsive reader group, have them look and give you suggestions. Just like we get our books edited, get a second or third set of eyes to review the content on your website.

Security – passwords/new technology advances

Passwords were mentioned in a previous lesson. I can't stress enough how important a strong password is for the security of your website. Just like you lock the door of your house to prevent random people from wandering in, you want a strong password to discourage the idle thief from wandering into your website and creating havoc.

We've all been told that passwords need to be changed periodically, but most of us don't actually do that. I had an author tell me that a constantly changing password adds too much stress to her life. I sympathize.

In the lesson on security, I encouraged you to invest in a password program. Worth every penny, I think. If you have a password program, changing your password is no longer a source of stress because the program keeps track of it. If you don't want to invest in a password program, try to set up a system of changing passwords that will make sense to you. I have an author who has a basic word for a password, and every three months adds a different string of numbers to the beginning of it. She knows the string of numbers are house numbers from previous places she has lived—but that isn't necessarily something that can be guessed by a stranger. See if you can create a similar system.

Regardless of what you set up, change your password to your website (and everywhere else!) once every 4 to 6 months. As I said previously, set a calendar reminder, set aside some time and get it done!

The other item that I've included in this section is "technology advances." I would include things like SSL in this grouping. Having a website involves staying somewhat in touch with the changes in technology. This is difficult for authors to do, as technology changes aren't really part of their normal world. Some of the larger author groups will periodically share informational blog posts or include items in their newsletters about this sort of information. I also include this sort of information in the newsletters I send out. Try to find a source of information and see if you can keep abreast of important developments.

Backups

I can't stress enough the necessity of backups. In a previous lesson we talked about this and I mentioned that every platform allows an export to be downloaded. This isn't the be all and end all, but it will contain the content of your website—the text and the pictures. Over the years I have fielded calls from authors—usually involving tears—about the loss of a website. My first question is about a backup and usually the answer is no. For all the websites I work on, the first thing I do is ensure that I have a backup. If something goes wrong during my work, I can put the backup in place and start again. It's like a little security blanket. I have noticed over the years that backups are a rare thing—therefore my harping on the subject!

If you have a WordPress.org site, put a plugin in place that will create automatic backups. And I encourage you to have those backups stored on cloud storage or somewhere other than your hosting company. Even if your hosting company does backups, do your own.

If you use a different platform than WordPress, set a memory minder, perhaps as I've suggested previously, a Google calendar alert – take an export of your site and store it somewhere safe. Back before I had access to automation, I used to back up every site after breakfast on Saturday mornings.

Whatever you decide to do—do it.

Updates

Updates are another thing that is overlooked. The majority of the platforms carry out updates for you. You might be notified that certain things have changed or get advanced warning of a service outage to install updates. If so, make sure that you look at the public side of your site after this has taken place. Most likely, nothing negative has happened, but this check only takes a minute or so and is a good use of your time.

WordPress.org is the platform where the updates are somewhat time consuming. As I mentioned in a previous lesson, the version of the WordPress program will require updating and plugins will require updating. Ignoring these updates creates potential security issues. I've covered how to update plugins on your site in a previous lesson. Periodically plugins are abandoned by their developers, especially free plugins. Because of this, I encourage you to set another memory minder, or Google calendar reminder, and check all your plugins to make sure they have been updated in the last year. This can be done every 6 to 9 months.

I hope all this sounds like something you can accomplish. Taking care of a website isn't generally a difficult job, but one that needs to be done.

CONCLUSION

I'd like to thank you for purchasing this book and working your way to the end! As I mentioned at the beginning, I look at websites differently than most authors. I'm sure that you realized that working your way through the content of the lessons.

I hope you have learned a lot of applicable lessons in this book and are able to make your author website the powerhouse that I know it can be.

I encourage you to sign up to my reader's group here: http://bakerviewconsulting.com to get periodic technical hints focused at the needs of authors delivered to your inbox.

If you learned something new from this book, please share your thoughts on the retailer you purchased a copy from!

Details of my books and courses can be found on the pages following the Glossary.

GLOSSARY

Balance – Contains equal amount of information, text, or graphics. Content that exists side by side starts and ends at the same point.

Blog – A blog is a type of website, which allows information to be added in a static fashion as well as a serial fashion. It can be run on a wide variety of platforms or programs.

Body – the main portion of a website or blog that sits below the header and above the footer. May be made up of one section of content or divided into several sections.

Browser – the program on a computer that is used to view websites. Examples are Chrome, Firefox, Safari, and Internet Explorer.

Cache – the memory of a browser program. Can be used as a verb —caching— indicating the saving of information about websites.

Clicks – When referring to stats, this section lets you know what visitors to your website click on.

Domain – also known as a URL—is the address of a website. It's typically in the format of http://yourdomainname.com (example http://barbdrozdowich.com)

Footer – The footer is the space at the very bottom of your website or blog. In some cases it can hold information in addition to a copyright statement.

Header – The Header is the part of a website at the top of the site and generally runs from side to side. It can also be used to refer to the top of a post, the area where the title is seen.

Hosting company – A Host or Hosting company is a business that has a collection of servers or big computers and sells/rents space on those servers for people to run a blog or website. Examples would be Site Ground, GoDaddy, or InMotion Hosting.

Hotlink – Hotlink is a common term to refer to a link that's attached to an image or some text in a website or blog. If a person clicks on that picture or text they are taken to another website. As an example, if a cover graphic of a book is "hotlinked" to an Amazon buy link or URL, when it's clicked on, the direct buy page for that book on Amazon is opened.

Landing page – the page of a website that is seen when the direct URL or domain of a website is used.

Location – where your visitors are located geographically. This may not be where you think.

Menu or Menu Bar – A Menu Bar is typically a line of clickable links either just under the header of a website/blog or in the header area of a website. The clickable links lead to other parts of the website or blog.

Mobile Responsive – refers to a website's ability to reorganize its content when viewed on a smaller screen—like a phone or a tablet.

Page Load – the speed with which a website loads (or appears)—typically measured in seconds and is dramatically affected by hosting, images and plugins.

Platform – the program that is used to operate a website. Examples are WordPress, Weebly, Blogger, and WIX.

Referrers – is the referring source of traffic to your website. It may be Facebook or Twitter, it may be another author's website, it may be a blogger's website. We want to keep track of friends and we want to know if actions on social media are sending visitors to our website.

RSS – Really Simple Syndication—the method many use to receive updates from a website/blog—is also know as a website's "feed"

Server – a fancy computer that houses the files for websites (typically many websites). Servers are usually owned by a business called a hosting company.

Sidebar – the area on one or both sides of a website or blog. It contains content that's placed there often in the form of widgets or gadgets.

SSL – Secure Socket Layer is a function a hosting company puts in place to signal your website has a secure connection to the internet.

Technology – what device your visitors are using to view your website.

Theme or Template – The code that controls the look and feel of a website. It typically controls the placement of content, the colors, the fonts, etc.

Time on site – from start to finish, how long, on average, your visitors are staying on your website. The longer the better!

Top Posts & Pages – is the list of the top (usually) 10 blog posts or pages that visitors are viewing.

URL – The direct link or address to a website or blog or a location on a website or a blog. It can be referred to as a Domain but can also be used to show the exact link to a specific entry on a website. (example: http://barbdrozdowich.com or http://barbdrozdowich/books)

Website – a site on the Internet.

ABOUT THE AUTHOR

Social Media and Wordpress Consultant Barb Drozdowich has taught in colleges, universities and in the banking industry. More recently, she brings her 15+ years of teaching experience and a deep love of books to help authors develop the social media platform needed to succeed in today's fast evolving publishing world. She delights in taking technical subjects and making them understandable by the average person. She owns Bakerview Consulting and manages the popular blog, Sugarbeat's Books, where she talks about Romance novels.

She is the author of 18 books, over 50 YouTube videos and an 5 online courses, all focused on helping authors and bloggers. Barb lives in the mountains of British Columbia with her family.

Barb can be found on her Book Blog, Business Blog, Pinterest, Goodreads, and Youtube

As well as:
barbdrozdowich.com
barb@bakerviewconsulting.com

ALSO BY BARB DROZDOWICH

All my books start with a problem that needs a solution - with a group of authors letting me know about a subject that they don't understand. I take it, break it down and see if I can add some clarity.

The books I've written attack the subjects of:

1) Understanding the world of Book Bloggers and Book Reviewers

2) Understanding all the parts and pieces of an author's online presence at a beginner's level

3) Understand the world of book promotions

4) Understanding What to blog, How to blog and Why to blog for authors

5) Understand how to use Goodreads as a tool of networking and communication with readers

6) Understand mailing lists and newsletters

7) Understand how to self-publish a book

During a recent workshop I gave on self-publishing, I walked participants through an exercise to help them understand the power of e-readers as well as the limits of e-readers. I was talking about the fact that not all e-readers can make use of clickable links as not all are connected to the internet or have browser capabilities. We also talked about creating links that readers from a variety of countries can actually use - my example was around solely using an Amazon.com link. Suddenly the light went in my own head about all of the clickable links I put in my books. So…going forward I'm directing everyone to a page that contains information about all of my books and buy links that are associated with those books. The link is easy to type in manually or click on if you have the ability. It is: https://readerlinks.com/mybooks/733

Below find a short description of each of my books and don't hesitate to use the link above to find out more information in terms of formats available and places to purchase a copy.

Below the description of the books, find descriptions of 4 online video courses that are available. All designed to address pain points that I hear from authors just like you.

The Authors Guide to Working with Book Bloggers

This book is the first book I wrote and is centered around information I received in a survey of book bloggers. This information has been updated through a second, more extensive survey. It is meant to serve as a primer for authors just entering the world of book bloggers or book reviewers. It helps explain the world of reviewers so that authors can walk confidently into that world and get some attention for a book.

More information: https://readerlinks.com/mybooks/733

The Author's On-Line Presence: How to find readers

This book attacks the subject of "what is an author's on-line presence?" Whether we use the word 'presence' or 'platform,' many beginner authors are intimidated by all the information swirling about the internet. The list of "must do" seems totally overwhelming. This book breaks down this subject into easy to understand chucks in normal language.

More information: https://readerlinks.com/mybooks/733

The Author's Guide to Book Promotions

This book was also borne out of many discussions with authors. What is a book blog tour? What is a promotional newsletter? How do I determine which promotion company to use? I break down the language and explain this world in easy to understand English. This book also has large lists of book tour companies as well as book promotion companies which will help you start your search.

More information: https://readerlinks.com/mybooks/733

An Author's Guide to Goodreads: How to Network with Millions of Readers

Goodreads seems to the site with so much power yet creates so much frustration in authors. I often describe this site as a rabbit's warren because of how difficult it is to navigate. This book will walk you through all aspects of how to effectively use Goodreads to communicate with readers. It also has a **Free course**

More information: https://readerlinks.com/mybooks/733

Top Advice for Authors Promoting Their Book and Book Blogger Survey

As I've mentioned previously, I've carried out several surveys of bloggers and written about the results. My first book, The Author's Guide to Working with Book Bloggers is the first book based on survey results. The two books pictured above are also based on survey results. The first one is simply the unfiltered collection of answers to the question: "If you could give an author one piece of advice about promoting their book, what would it be?" This book lists all 500+ responses. The second book is a full analysis of all 30+ questions. If you are interested in finding out real information about the book blogging/book reviewer world, these books will help.

More information: https://readerlinks.com/mybooks/733

The Complete Mailing List Toolkit

I like to say that this book covers mailing lists and newsletters from soup to nuts. It doesn't focus on one aspect of communicating with readers, it covers it all. Each section is available individually and this book also has a free course associated with it.

More information: https://readerlinks.com/mybooks/733

The Author's Guide to Self-Publishing For Canadians and How to Self-Publish a Book

Both of these books are quite similar in terms of content. I really wanted to write a book focused at self-publishing for my fellow Canadians - hence the first book. The second book is similar content but without the specific Canadian content. The references are applicable for writers in any country.

More information: https://readerlinks.com/mybooks/733

On-Line Video Courses:

WordPress for Beginners

Are you an author or blogger who struggles with the technical side of your website? Do you wish you could change the layout of your website but are afraid you'll break it?

In "WordPress for Beginners," you'll learn how to build a beautiful, functional website in WordPress. This course is designed just for authors or bloggers who have little to no technical experience, so you don't need any prior knowledge. Your instructor, Barb Drozdowich, uses easy-to-follow directions with specific examples so you'll be able to get started on your website right away.

When you sign up for "WordPress for Beginners," you'll get immediate access to more than 8 hours of content covering topics such as:

- Choosing a hosting company and get your website going
- Understanding the basics of WordPress: logging in, layouts, settings, etc.
- Using themes and plugins
- Protecting your site from hackers and spammers
- Making sure your website looks great on any browser or phone
- Backing up your website

Once you have the basics down, there are even a few advanced topics to build upon what you've learned, like using Google Analytics to track your content performance and setting up search engine optimization (SEO).

If you are an author or blogger looking to build a brand-new website or enhance the one you already have, don't let your lack of confidence stop you. Sign up and get started on that shiny new site today!

https://the-author-s-technical-help-desk.teachable.com/p/wordpress-for-beginners

WordPress Dot Com for Beginners

Whether you're looking to start a blog or put together a website for your small business, figuring out how to actually get going can feel like a tall task.

But it doesn't have to be.

In "WordPress.com for Beginners," you'll learn everything you need to know to get a website up and running on the free version of WordPress. The course includes 25 easy-to-understand videos that guide you through each step, from creating an account to setting up your site to publishing your first post.

When you sign up for "WordPress.com for Beginners," you'll get immediate access to more than 3 hours of content covering topics such as:

- Setting up your WordPress.com account
- The difference between pages and posts and how to publish content on them
- A walk-through of 4 different themes and how to use them on your website
- How to manage comments and give other people access to your website
- What are widgets and how can they improve your site

There are even a few freebies and plenty of other resources along the way to set you up for success.

If you've made the decision to launch your own website, don't let the technology scare you away. Sign up today and start publishing your content in no time!

https://the-author-s-technical-help-desk.teachable.com/p/wordpress-com-for-beginners

Mailerlite for Beginners

If you sell a product or offer a service, you should also have a mailing list. It's the best way to get information out to your audience, share offers, and turn enthusiastic fans into paying customers. People who have signed up for your newsletter are already interested in what you have to say and are much more likely to pay attention to what you have to offer than if they stumble across an ad on social media.

Once you start collecting email addresses, you'll want to sign up for a newsletter service that can send customized emails to multiple people at a time.

In "Mailerlite for Beginners," you'll learn all about one of the simpler newsletter services, Mailerlite. Your instructor, Barb Drozdowich, will walk you through the steps from how to navigate the dashboard, how to create a campaign (a newsletter), how to create signup forms, and more.

When you sign up, you'll have immediate access to 19 videos that cover everything you need to know to get started, such as:

• The legalities you need to know about (opt-ins and opt-outs, what the GDPR is and what it means for you)

• How to set up your account

• Managing your subscribers

• How to create a campaign and send out a newsletter

• How to run reports to see what percentage of people are opening your emails and clicking on the links within your newsletters

You'll also get plenty of resources for more information and support once the course is over.

Learning something new can feel overwhelming, but it doesn't have to be. Sign up and start connecting with your potential customers today!

https://the-author-s-technical-help-desk.teachable.com/p/mailerlite-for-beginners

How to Self-Publish a Book

Each year, more and more authors are realizing that they don't have to take the traditional publishing route to get their work out into the world. Self-publishing is a great option for many writers, but the actual process of publishing a book yourself can feel overwhelming.

So overwhelming that you might not ever get started in the first place.

In "How to Self-Publish a Book," you'll learn everything from putting together your manuscript to getting an ISBN number to formatting and distributing your book. The easy-to-understand, step-by-step format will guide you through the entire process. Before you know it, you'll be sharing your brand new book with your friends and family!

When you sign up for "How to Self-Publish a Book", you'll get immediate access to 19 videos (more than two hours of content!) that cover key topics such as:

- How the publishing industry has changed and what that means for potential authors
- All aspects of publishing: Writing, editing, designing, formatting, uploading, marketing
- What you need to know about file formats
- The necessary pieces to include in a book file
- Where to sell your book
- Red flags to look for if you go with a self-publishing service

Plus, plenty of additional links and resources along the way for even more information.

Don't let what you don't know stop you. Sign up today and finally become the published author you've always dreamed of!

https://the-author-s-technical-help-desk.teachable.com/p/how-to-publish-a-book

www.ingramcontent.com/pod-product-compliance
Lightning Source LLC
Chambersburg PA
CBHW071856070526
44583CB00016B/1714